THE REAL
DOWNTON
ABBEY

THE REAL
DOWNTON
ABBEY

AN UNOFFICIAL GUIDE TO
THE PERIOD WHICH INSPIRED
THE HIT TV SHOW

JACKY HYAMS

JOHN BLAKE

Published by John Blake Publishing Ltd,
3 Bramber Court, 2 Bramber Road,
London W14 9PB, England

www.johnblakepublishing.co.uk

www.facebook.com/Johnblakepub   facebook

twitter.com/johnblakepub   twitter

First published in paperback in 2011

ISBN: 978 1 84358 404 9

British Library Cataloguing-in-Publication Data:

A catalogue record for this book is available from the British Library.

Design by www.envydesign.co.uk

Printed and bound by CPI Group (UK) Ltd, Croydon CR0 4YY

1 3 5 7 9 10 8 6 4 2

Papers used by John Blake Publishing are natural, recyclable products made
from wood grown in sustainable forests. The manufacturing processes conform
to the environmental regulations of the country of origin.

Every attempt has been made to contact the relevant copyright-holders,
but some were unobtainable. We would be grateful if the
appropriate people could contact us.

Author's Note

B efore 1971 the pound was divided into twenty shillings (s); one shilling was made up of twelve pennies (d). 240 pennies made up £1. A guinea was worth 21 shillings (or £1 and one shilling).

I have given many prices and sums of money in the original currency. In order to calculate today's value of any original price quoted, the National Archives has a very useful website with a currency calculator *(www.nationalarchives.gov.uk/currency)*.

Acknowledgements

S incere thanks for their valuable insights and generosity with
their time go to Joy Meir, Laura Mason, Jeremy Musson,
David Trevor-Jones, Kerry Bristol and Sarah Tobias.

For more information on English country houses and
domestic service, I can recommend the following: *The Country
House Servant* by Pamela A. Sambrook (Sutton Publishing,
1999); *Keeping Their Place* by Pamela A. Sambrook (The History
Press, 2007); *Up and Down Stairs* by Jeremy Musson (John
Murray, 2010); and *Not in Front of the Servants* by Frank Victor
Dawes (Century, 1991).

Contents

Introduction

The horse-drawn State Landau slowly makes its way from Westminster Abbey towards St James's Park. Inside the open carriage, the handsome prince in his scarlet tunic and his beautiful new bride wave delightedly at the crowds noisily cheering them on. Colourfully attired footmen ride behind them. Close your eyes briefly and you could be back in 1902, the year the carriage was built for King Edward VII. But we're here, in the twenty-first century, on a beautiful spring day when British history, ceremonial pomp, brilliant pageantry and a spectacular display of centuries-old tradition briefly capture the whole world's attention. Royalty and privilege. They may no longer be relevant to our lives in any way, but when they're put on very public display it's impossible not to be fascinated by our past.

The same applies to TV historical or costume drama. We're fascinated by it because it shows us such different worlds to our twenty-first century lives. Fictional TV series like *Downton*

Abbey, Upstairs Downstairs, or the movie, *The King's Speech,* are compelling because they tell us so much about our history. With their precise attention to every detail, they give us many tantalising insights into the worlds of royalty, the rich, the privileged of the time — and, of course, those that worked to serve them.

This bird's-eye view of the day-to-day lives of the live-in servants, their subservience to the super-rich, their personal dramas and the everyday restrictions of their lives, creates an irresistible blend of history and fiction. And, of course, what makes the sumptuous *Downton Abbey* world of toffs and servants even more compelling is its very proximity in time to today; we're not looking at the very distant past here. These lives, so different from our own in every way and lived in an atmosphere of amazing wealth, extreme formality and snobbery, stuffy convention, etiquette — and unbelievable servitude — were lived just over a hundred years ago.

But why are we so fascinated by the master-servant relationship itself? Part of the reason may be because we now feel that much closer to it because we can access our knowledge of it ourselves. We are continually encouraged to locate our own history, track down our own past. And it's so easy. Digging into the lives of our families via information published online and websites like Ancestry.com reveals so much to us now at the push of a button. We may not have distant aristocratic relations in our family tree — the aristocrats are very much a minority group — but many of us are now discovering that we have relatives, great grandparents, distant aunts, uncles or cousins, who went into service and lived in the grand house; relatives that scrubbed, cooked and cleaned for the wealthy family with their vast estates and snobbish ways.

Just before I finished this book, a friend mentioned to me that his eighty-something mother had clear and coherent recollections of her own mother's life as a cook in a big Scottish country house in the early 1900s. As was typical then, she left the job to get married. Photos of my friend's grandmother as a beautiful young woman, wearing her servant's apron, popped into my email inbox. Would she talk to me? Sadly not. She wanted to. But without a letter of permission from the descendants of her mother's employers, she said, she dare not speak out. It wouldn't be right. The cap-doffing traditions of servitude still, to this day, linger on in the minds of the living.

So who were these toffs and servants that hold so much fascination for us? How did they live, what did they wear, what did they eat, how did they play or form relationships – and how much – or how little – did they spend or earn? In this book I answer many of these questions and reveal, too, a lot more about what went on behind those huge front doors to the grand country house.

It was obvious before I started writing that there was a vast contrast between the two worlds of aristocrats and servants. But as I made my way through the different aspects of their lives, I discovered that the contrast was even starker than I'd imagined. A closer look at the strict social etiquette and the rules of this class-bound period gives you a powerful appreciation of today's freedoms. Time and again the same question crops up: how could women, in particular, accept all the restriction and regulation of so much of their lives?

No one would envy the servants their slog and daily lives ruled by their employers' whims where, for example, a young servant girl could not openly conduct a relationship with a boyfriend or admirer unless she had a very enlightened employer. The 'No Followers' rule of the period is unthinkable nowadays. Nor can we envisage a world where marriage spelt the end of a job or any sort of working life. Yet that is how it was for millions of women little more than a century ago. What we take for granted, our unquestionable freedom of choice, didn't exist for them.

At the other end of the scale, the wealthy, privileged women who might, at first glance, seem enviably to have it all, with servants running back and forth to satisfy every tiny whim and trunkloads of the finest expensive designer gear shipped in from Paris whenever they wanted, were equally restricted by their class and exalted position in society – but in a very different way. They could only be married. They could not divorce (divorce equalled shame and rejection in their world), and they couldn't remain single (spinster equalled another kind of social reject). And there were servants around them every minute of their lives. There was no privacy as we know it: they were in a gilded, very beautiful cage.

This is where the fictional TV version of the era *Downton Abbey* mirrors the reality of those times so precisely. Many of the older, grand women – the Duchess of Grantham in particular, as recreated so beautifully by Maggie Smith – are determinedly snobbish and class conscious. In the real world outside their gilded backdrop, a major storm is starting to break: society is now rejecting the political supremacy of the ruling class and starting to give the working person a voice. Change is the last thing her generation wishes to contemplate. Yet her granddaughter, Lady Sybil, aware of this impending social storm, attempts at least, to get involved and attends a protest meeting – and she helps one of the servants find a less restrictive job in an office.

Make no mistake, the Edwardian years before World War I broke out were times of real social upheaval: the Suffrage Movement, increasingly violent and dramatic, drew much attention to the fact that women could not vote – although it wasn't until 1928 that the vote was given to all women.

Despite the efforts of the reforming Liberal Government

and Prime Minister Herbert Asquith, in the years between 1911 and 1914 there was considerable industrial unrest across the country. Yet the years between 1900 and 1914 were ushering in many reforms and the beginnings of a welfare state: the needs of the ordinary person were no longer going to be ignored.

Politics aside, there is another reason why we're so drawn to the lives of the previous century: we're immersed in the idea that we live in a 'classless society' yet somehow, we're a bit uneasy about it. So we're intrigued by a world where everyone 'knows their place' because everything, for them, is so clearly prescribed or set down. And, of course, we continue to live with them. The evidence of Edwardian life is everywhere. Not only the big department stores, hotels, theatres and seaside resorts where they enjoyed themselves, but our homes too. The Edwardians and Victorians built so much housing that still stands in our country. Servants worked for millions of middle-class families in cities too, not just the super-rich country house dwellers. So anyone living in a house or conversion from the Victorian or Edwardian era inhabits the same space, may see the same view from their window. Climb the many flights of stairs to the tiny bedroom at the very top of the house and there is the servant's world: the tiny fireplace, the narrow single bed and bare wooden floorboards. We can easily imagine their lives for ourselves. Maybe that's why they are so real to us.

More insights to these lives can also be found, of course, in taking time out to visit the grand country houses dotted all over the country, many open to the general public, thanks to their owners and the work of English Heritage and the National Trust. These houses are awesome examples of architectural grandeur, wealth, and the long histories of many aristocratic families. Some houses show, in some detail, the fascinating insights into life below stairs, so that we can see with our own eyes how it was, wander around their vast gardens and estates and gaze at the impressive splendour of their vast interiors.

Downton Abbey starts in 1912 with the sinking of the *Titanic*, two years before World War I erupts. This book covers a wider period, from the late 1800s right up to 1914 when the war started.

Technically, the Edwardian period starts at the beginning of 1901 when Queen Victoria died and her eldest son, 'Bertie', Prince of Wales, took the throne until he too died in 1910. But although Edward VII's reign is brief, less than ten years before his son George became King George V in 1910, the term Edwardian is used to describe the entire period after Queen Victoria died up to 1914, mainly because it is so closely linked to the opulence, elegance and sophistication of the ruling aristocratic class who surrounded Edward VII – the elite whose waning influence marked the beginning of the end of the rigid class system that dominated millions of lives for hundreds of years.

We left the world of toffs and servants when the next page of history was turned, the onset of World War I in August 1914. After this, many grand country houses were requisitioned as hospitals to treat the sick and wounded. This war with Germany – 'a war to end all wars' – destroyed many lives. Close to a million British men were killed and millions more wounded in combat – yet it eventually sped up the process of the changes in society that were already beginning to be felt before the war. Wealthy, privileged individuals took up arms alongside ordinary working men: unbreakable bonds, irrelevant of class or background, were formed in adversity – and after the war, they remained, helping bring the class barriers down.

Women too, took on new roles in place of the men away fighting; in peace time, they didn't want to relinquish their recently- found freedoms and, most importantly, as they came through the disruption and chaos of war, working people started to see that they no longer had to toil away all their lives to support the lifestyle of the rich or privileged.

Servants didn't suddenly fade away overnight, of course. But the figures speak for themselves: a life in service no longer appealed to successive generations with other work options. And the decline of aristocratic wealth meant those in servitude themselves were no longer needed in large numbers. By 1931 there were 1.3 million servants in domestic employment in Britain, 700,000 less than at the beginning of the century. In 1951, following World War II, there were just 250,000 such workers in Britain. And a decade on, in 1961, just 100,000 people worked as servants. The wider availability of labour-saving household devices, better job opportunities and wider education options for all, in time, limited the availability or need for servants.

Today, the well-off continue to hire domestic help around the house and in the garden, to drive them around, look after their children or work in any way that may be needed. Agencies who specialise in supplying experienced butlers on a full- or part-time basis continue to thrive. Housekeepers are still hired to run households for the rich. And some people still opt to have live-in help in their home. But, generally, the relationship between employer and employee tends to be quite different.

Sometimes, the disgruntled servant will simply sack the master. Only the other day, a friend told me she'd lost her long-term cleaner. 'She gave me the sack – by text message,' she wailed.

That, for me, sums it all up. Today's domestic servants may need the cash – but essentially they're free in a way that could never have been imagined a century ago. She or he can sack the boss if they want to. And in this world, thankfully, there are no 'Servants' Rules' to worry about.

Chapter 1

The House

It stands at the end of a long, winding gravel driveway, set in five thousand acres of perfectly landscaped parklands. It's the grandest of grand houses, built from honey-coloured Bath stone, a monument to the wealth, privilege and history of the titled family that has owned this house and the land around it for centuries.

Step inside the massive and imposing studded wooden doors into a vast, breathtaking entrance hall with wide, tiled floors, enormous columns and neck-craning vaulted ceilings.

Climb the equally imposing staircase with their polished oak balustrades and gaze, in awe, at the splendour and opulence of the interiors and the furnishings: the saloon with its towering ceilings, the enormous library displaying thousands of valuable antique books, the stunning drawing room with silk-covered walls and curtains, the vast, gilded huge double doors leading to the beautifully furnished smoking room hung with valuable works of art, the enchanting music room with its baroque painted ceiling and walls decorated with sixteenth-century Italian embroideries, room after room displaying the evidence of a magnificently elegant and sumptuous way of life.

Venture above these vast State Rooms and you find more than fifty bedrooms, where the rich and privileged owners once played host to the many impeccably attired, equally wealthy house guests that were such an important part of their social life in the early twentieth century.

This is Highclere Castle in Berkshire. This Victorian gothic pile, home to the Carnarvon family since 1679 and rebuilt in the eighteenth and nineteenth centuries, is the stunningly beautiful location for the TV series *Downton Abbey*, set in the Edwardian era in the early years of the 1900s. Back in 1912, when the story of Downton Abbey starts, Highclere had close to thirty servants working there.

Across the UK, we can still visit and explore many other examples of Britain's architectural heritage: grand, vast country houses and estates like this, some with hundreds of rooms, every estate with a proud aristocratic history going back many centuries, each one with a fascinating story to tell.

But as lovers of the TV series will know, the story of this house is not just about the fabulous setting, the grand design, our fascination with history and the trappings of immense wealth and great aristocratic privilege. For the story behind this elegantly appointed country home – and others like it – is a very human one about the people, the men and women living behind the imposing doors, their dreams, their disappointments, their hopes and their fears for themselves and their loved ones. Love, lust, deceit, duplicity and sorrow, the all-too-common elements of human experience, can be found within these majestic surrounds, even though the inhabitants of such houses, the masters and their servants, occupied very different roles in the world they lived in – and for convention and tradition's sake frequently concealed or hid their innermost feelings or emotions.

The rigid class system that once ruled British society and the lives of the population was about to disintegrate in the 'Downton era', the early pre-World War I years of the twentieth century when modern Britain, as we now know it, was born. Yet the social divisions between the occupants of houses like these, bred over centuries of tradition and restriction in ways unimaginable to us, continued to remain in place in this era, as they had always been, frozen in time; attitudes and traditions where stifling restriction and rules of etiquette dominated everything, an unequal world where personal freedoms were still limited by strict social boundaries for rich and poor alike.

Move away, by design or chance, from these rigidly harsh restrictive lines and you risked everything. For the rich, stepping outside the boundaries primarily meant loss of social status, their closely guarded, highly esteemed place in the highest pecking order – though a very wealthy woman often had most to lose if she fell from social grace and was shunned or ostracised by her peer group. Yet for the servants of the upper classes, male or female, a breach of the rules – and a sacking – in a vastly unequal world could mean total ruin, abject poverty – or even starvation on the streets. That's how vast the gulf was between them.

In the upper floors of this grand mansion, inhabiting vast luxuriously appointed spaces, lived the pampered, leisured upper-crust ladies and gentlemen and their families, their everyday lives dominated by centuries-old snobbery, convention and immense inherited wealth.

Today, most of us splash out on an exotic holiday in a far-off destination for a taste of luxury, being waited on, having whatever we want for an all-too-brief time. Yet many of the early twentieth-century country-house owners, like the fictional Earl of Grantham and his family, wallowed in luxurious living every day of their gilded lives.

Far below them, in more ways than one, tucked away in the hidden reaches of the big house, sometimes in cramped living quarters – and frequently invisible to outsiders and even their own masters – were their live-in servants, constantly at the beck and call of their masters who never needed to lift a finger to do anything for themselves – other than following a carefully mapped routine of grand entertaining, eating, visiting friends and relatives, running their estates and pursuing socially acceptable pursuits or outdoor activities.

The irony is that the two groups can't survive without each other. The country house servant classes worked, sometimes virtually round the clock, for a mere pittance, their sole means of survival. Yet it was only their crushingly relentless toil, often backbreaking and physically tough, that enabled their masters and mistresses to live such smoothly run, cushioned, lives of luxury – for without servant labour such a house and the land surrounding it couldn't function properly at all.

A visitor to the house in the early 1900s sees an incredibly well run, perfectly organised endeavour. Wealthy foreign visitors at this time sometimes marvelled at the amazingly well-organised way the English country house was run. But the truth is it can only work so well for one reason: the long established day-in, day-out hard work of the smaller cogs in the massive wheel, those who do the fetching, carrying, dusting, rubbing, polishing, heaving, cleaning, washing, gardening and many more complex tasks, scurrying to obey each and every command or summons from their masters' bells.

This army of servants is the hidden element in the enterprise that ultimately gives the house its air of serene, leisured opulence. Even though equality between the sexes and the classes is now ahead on the horizon, here, among the rich, leisured classes, it still seems a long way off.

So who are they, these two groups of people whose lives are ruled, 24/7 by class and birth, the opposing ends of the social spectrum? And how do they come to be living this way in the early years of the twentieth century? Before we take a look at the many different aspects of their day-to-day lives, let's take a closer look behind the grand façade to find out more about who these people are and how they got here...

THE TOFFS

The families that own the vast country house estates during this period are in one sense an elite power group, part of a super-rich ruling class of land-owning aristocracy and high-born gentry that have remained at the very epicentre of power and royal patronage in Britain for hundreds of years.

Effectively, they are a ruling class, around 10,000 people from 1,500 families whose privilege, ancient lineage and wealth has kept them at the top of society for hundreds of years.

Aristocrats, where the head of a family might be a knight or a baronet, hold the very highest political influence and power in government. And they own 90 per cent of the nation's land, much of it in vast, sprawling estates. As a result, their wealth, frequently handed down to the eldest son over the centuries, is immense: large country house estates valued at over £5 million (around £300 million in today's money) were not unknown in the years just before 1914.

But it doesn't stop there. These multi-million pound vast country homes are also continuous and awesomely impressive power bases for social networking, places for relaxing, extravagant dining, hunting and shooting parties with their owners' wealthy equals, other aristocrats and royalty, once the cares of running the country are set aside. Moreover, some of these homes have been created, at huge expense and usually by 'new' money (the millions earned by entrepreneurs in trade, shipping or mining, rather than 'old' money, i.e. inherited wealth) as a showcase for their owner's wealth and top-notch status, with big collections of priceless art, luxurious furnishings and enormous and perfectly tended gardens and tennis courts.

Some of these aristocrats own grand town houses too – located in specific upmarket areas like Piccadilly, St James's Square or Park Lane in London: only the 'right' address will maintain the upper-crust profile, postcode snobbery of the highest order. Others own more than one estate, so they may frequently move around the country, visiting each one, according to the time of year.

As a result, huge numbers of servants have, by tradition, always been needed to work and run these mini empires: think of the many hundreds of thousands of people employed by Britain's big supermarkets and you get some idea of the scale of the Edwardian landowners' power as employers and bosses. So not only do the elite, exclusive group of aristocrats, gentry and highly esteemed members of the House of Lords run the country – they have been, for centuries, its greatest providers of work, perhaps the biggest employers in their area, keeping hundreds of servants and workers in employment.

But these earls, knights and duchesses, once supremely confident of their prime position in the pecking order, are having to confront unsettling changes in the world around them. None of these changes have happened overnight. But the march of progress and the spectre of war are about to topple their pre-eminence.

And so as the storm cloud of World War I starts to gather over their gilded world, the decline of their once overwhelming influence – through what comes to be known as a 'golden' era –

accelerates. Essentially, this is the slow beginning of the end of their tightly held reign over society, the extreme rule of privilege and wealth.

THE POWER SHIFT: HOW DID IT HAPPEN?

The shift in the power of the aristocratic elite started half a century before in the mid-1800s with the massive industrial revolution of the Victorian era and the early beginnings of what we now know as modern industry and the consumer society.

Until then, the poorest people faced limited employment options other than as agricultural rural workers or in service. But these big changes start, over time, to provide alternative means of employment for large numbers of people in mills, factories, railroads and shops. And eventually, as people begin to have greater mobility to move around – an important factor in the growth of Britain's economy – a slow but steady shift evolves in the ways people live and work.

Bit by bit, decade by decade, the rich and powerful elite landowners find themselves under fire, criticised for their treatment of the poor – and for the shocking inequalities of a society where this 10 per cent of the British population own 92 per cent of the country's wealth.

Taxation is also starting to be a bit of a headache for the ruling classes, nibbling away at their inheritances. Death duties on their estates, introduced in 1894, come on the heels of a long agricultural recession brought on because Britain has started to import more foodstuffs, thereby bringing down local agricultural prices. And this, in turn, reduces the value of land in the great estates – a late nineteenth-century property slump, if you like.

Some of the wealthy ruling class have huge debts to pay and they start to sell off their estates – or, if they own several country houses, some of their houses. Following continuous political pressure to increase the taxes paid by the very richest landowners, in 1909 the 'people's budget', championed by the Liberal Chancellor of the Exchequer Lloyd George, introduces big tax increases for the most wealthy people in society.

Country-house owners at this time already paid tax for each male servant they employed (this started in 1777 and didn't end until 1937), but the servant tax did not apply to female servants, who were much cheaper to employ anyway. So by the early twentieth century, the big country households had already undergone their own version of cutbacks, starting with their wages bill – often the biggest expense when running their big estates. They'd already been replacing male servants with cheaper females; previously traditional male servant roles like house stewards, hall ushers and grooms of the chamber were gradually replaced in the late 1800s by the butler, the housekeeper and the parlour maid. In some cases, footmen too were replaced – by housemaids. And by now, only the really great households continue to employ the more expensive male cooks. The hard-working and harassed cook, Mrs Patmore (Lesley Nicol), heading up the Downton kitchen might well have learned her duties as a kitchen maid working for a temperamental male chef with better take-home pay.

Technology too has started to influence the way the rich live: the motorcar is not reliable or even widely accepted by 1900 – but cars gradually become commonplace for the wealthy over the next few years, with the chauffeur replacing the coachman. As a result of these changes in technology, less manual labour is required in some houses.

Yet as badly paid as they are by our standards, by the early twentieth century domestic servants are getting slightly more expensive and not quite as easy to recruit as in the past, partly thanks to the growth and development of towns and cities, which eventually creates more job options for the working classes in shops, factories and offices.

Even so, most of the big country houses are still well staffed, an average of about twenty to thirty indoor servants living in each house. And the need everywhere for servants remains consistent: large numbers of them work for middle-class families in the big cities. Only the very poorest people cannot afford some sort of servant or domestic help.

Yet although the middle class tend to have far fewer servants for their smaller households, they too are often finding it difficult to employ and retain good servants: youngsters from the poorest backgrounds who might have willingly followed their relatives into an entire life working in service for the wealthy, generation after generation, are now actively starting to question this: some realise that there are different, less restrictive, ways of earning a crust other than being a live-in servant, even if the wages are low.

However the biggest power shift that is nudging the aristocracy from their lofty perch is that they are no longer the only rich kids on the block. With the English industrial revolution of the mid-1800s and the expansion of the British Empire – which spanned a quarter of the globe at its height – comes the gradual rise of the moneyed industrialists, the factory and mill owners, a new breed of get-up-and-go entrepreneurs. The Richard Bransons of their day, they are making millions from overseas trade, coal mining, shipping and cloth, rather than mere inheritance handed down from generation to generation. Some aristocratic country-house owners have benefited from this, of course, because they already own huge tracts of land ready to be developed as the towns and cities expand.

But the ever-growing spending power and influence of the

new entrepreneurs – combined with the influential voice of the professional middle classes – is starting to unseat the snobbish, class-bound aristocrats who now have to face facts: they can no longer afford to shun or ignore the existence – or the company – of equally wealthy people who may have started life without an ancient name or high-born lineage – but who, through their own endeavours, can easily match the aristos' spending power.

Some wealthy industrialists have also started to buy into the aristocrat's way of life, building vast houses and estates of their own, sometimes with all the latest mod cons; a few have installed their own heating system, electrical plant, telephone network – and a telegrapher to send off urgent telegrams.

While the more conservative players in the aristocratic world don't always rush to adopt the latest new technologies like electricity – some country-house owners are extremely reluctant to change rooms designed for oil lamps and candlelight – the penny is starting to drop: other people can – and do – match their vast influence. And some of these 'new money' people have started to marry into the aristocracy, a clear case of 'if you can't beat 'em – join 'em'.

Despite the big role that even the pleasure-loving King, Edward VII, has already played in introducing the aristocrats to the 'nouveaux riches' (the new rich) via lavish entertainments, trips abroad and expensive parties in an attempt to smooth away the rough edges of this transition, extreme snobbery about where money comes from still lingers over certain sections of the country-house world.

Super-snobs like the Dowager Duchess of Grantham (Maggie Smith) who can't tolerate the idea of the family wealth being in the hands of a middle-class heir – a mere Manchester solicitor who actually earns his money and prefers not to have a team of servants fussing over him – underline the reality of the toffs' position: their supremacy as masters of all they survey is all but over. And it hurts.

But as we will see, by the way they continue to live – and party – you'd never have guessed the storm was coming.

THE SERVANT CLASS SYSTEM

This incredible class divide where everyone 'knows their place' and has a firmly set series of tasks to perform day-in, day-out, is not just a division between the two groups, master and live-in servant. For such is the long-established country house servant tradition – in Tudor times a noble with a vast country estate might have hundreds of staff working for him – that even in the early 1900s, when the British class system is already beginning to buckle, there is frequently a hierarchy amongst domestic staff, two separate servant classes living under one roof. Three very distinct groups of people all labouring and living under the same roof in the big country house or within its vast surrounds.

First in the pecking order are the upper servants, an experienced group of well-drilled slightly older professionals with specific areas of responsibility and direct, if usually formal, access to their employers. (In some instances they will have to make an appointment to talk to their master or mistresses.)

Then, way beneath them in status – even applying to the areas of the house they sleep in – is the second tier, the lower servants, frequently younger, 'invisible' workers, some of whom virtually work as servants for the upper group.

The harsh and rigid line dividing the two servant classes may only be crossed by the lowers in one way: hard work – strict adherence to all the restrictive rules and regulations governing a life in service and complete, unstinting deference to both their masters and the upper servants, from whom the lowers learn the ropes. Careful behaviour and steady, if gruelling, toil for years can eventually mean a move up to the higher servant ranks. Promotion. Of a sort. Because while the upper-class of servants live more comfortably, often with their own live-in quarters, earn more (but not much more) and have far greater access to their employers' private lives – and their darkest secrets – theirs is still a working life of rigid formality, unstinting routine and furious bursts of planned activity when large groups of rich and famous guests are due to be entertained or the family go travelling – and very little else.

OK, it represents a steady job for life for many, at a time when the majority of the population are living in less than luxury (and the upper echelon of servants can sometimes be just as snobbish about their position in life as their masters). But this is definitely not anything like a working life as we might recognise it.

THE SERVANTS

The size of the very grand country house varies from estate to estate. Yet the working traditions of these houses remained pretty much the same over hundreds of years. Anyone who worked as a servant in a big country house remained a servant: that was it. Provided you stayed employed, of course.

By 1901, an estimated two million people work as domestic servants (out of a total population of 40 million). Many of the servants working in the biggest, grandest houses continue to be drawn from a vast pool of poverty stricken, sometimes rural families: in some areas, successive generations have been working for a local aristocrat for centuries, a long-standing means of survival for millions in a harshly delineated existence.

Mostly, though, their education has been restricted. Although the official school-leaving age in Edwardian times is

13, attendance by poorer children is frequently haphazard, simply because so many have to work to help provide for their family. Even the brightest poverty-stricken child has no option other than to work, if circumstances dictate, rather than study.

Literacy, however, is now becoming important: employers prefer to take on servants who can read, write and add up. In some cases, poorer people have become more literate since the late 1800s. But there are still huge discrepancies in people's knowledge. A young, illiterate girl entering service at the lowest level is at a distinct disadvantage with scant chance of promotion: there's a great deal of paperwork involved in running a country house: archives show lots of bills, accounts, letters, inventories. A cook or her assistant should be able to read and write a menu, for instance. And if a servant can't write properly, they can't even communicate with their own family should they find themselves working some distance away from home. The consequences of poverty, such as malnutrition, poor health and lack of communication skills, don't exactly help anyone's prospects if they follow a life in service.

And, of course, poverty itself continues to cast a terrible shadow over Edwardian families as it did in Victorian times; a family of ten children or more could be reduced to the breadline – or worse, the workhouse, where the very poorest in society wind up – if its sole wage earner, a working father, dies or becomes too sick or injured to keep working.

So most Edwardian country-house servants begin their working life at a very low social level indeed. Perhaps bitter and twisted sneaky lady's maid O'Brien (Siobhan Finneran) got that way because she started her working life in another country house in the same job as Daisy (Sophie McShera), the lowliest scullery maid, the person with the hardest and worst job in the household.

Yet despite all the drawbacks, even a low-ranking post in a

big country house is regarded as a better job prospect than being a live-in servant for a middle-class family in the city. First of all, working for the upper-crust rich families in their country residences is seen as being of a higher social status, rather than working for comfortable but less-affluent middle-class families in a smaller house in town.

Then there's the practical consideration: more space. Town or city servants don't always get much of a deal in terms of accommodation because their work in smaller homes frequently means they have to sleep in very cramped conditions, often right next to their place of work. In a London house, for instance, an under butler might sleep in the butler's pantry. Or a footman will sleep in a basement.

Since country-house servants already come from pokey and overcrowded homes housing many children – where even having a bed to yourself is a luxury only to be dreamed of – sleeping conditions in big country houses can sometimes be better. A young female servant, for instance, starts off in service sleeping in a sparsely furnished attic room, usually a hard-to-reach dormitory at the very top of the house (sometimes known as 'the convent'), which she shares with six or more other young girls. Sometimes she might have to share a tiny bed with another girl.

Servants' sleeping quarters are rigidly segregated. The general idea is to keep the young women away from the attentions of all men; not just the more lecherous employers (the sons and heirs) but the other male servants too. So the servants' quarters have completely separate staircases and entrances, sometimes overlooked by the butler or house-keeper's rooms.

The back stairs of the house and the servants' entrance at the rear of the property (the place where all household deliveries are made) is only to be used by the servants – at all times. In fact, the only time the domestic staff are allowed anywhere near the main staircase in the house – used only by the family and their guests – is when they are actually doing their job of cleaning or dusting it. And, of course, they must never ever be seen by their bosses, they are an invisible army of manual labour, sweeping and dusting, polishing and cleaning, often while the family are asleep.

And if they need to clean a room, for any reason at all, they are only permitted to work in it if anyone in the family is not scheduled to use it. What this means is that a lower servant can wind up working in the same country house for years, yet not once will they come into contact with a member of the family they work for.

Yet despite all these restrictions, a tiny narrow bed in a room shared with many others might well be an improvement on the poverty-stricken environment of their own family home.

Some country-house archive inventories show that in exceptional cases, live-in servants slept in feather beds – on wool mattresses. But usually the sleeping facilities are very spartan and the dormitory accommodation has very little furnishing, bare wooden floors and not much more. Washing facilities in the dormitory are usually limited to a basin and a jug of water on a stand and, of course, toilets are shared with many others – and are not always close to the chilly dormitories. A zinc or copper hip bath might also be located separately in a servants' bathroom for their use or, in a few cases, in the communal sleeping quarters – but usually, on rising, it's just a case of a quick splash from the water jug.

In the newer, more recently built big country houses, the layout is more thoughtfully planned: many rooms are allocated to specific household tasks in order to make the management of the house easier. (This follows a general trend of grand and wealthy households where the rooms they use often have one function only.) These areas of the household, let's call them task rooms, might be allocated to side courts in the house, rather than the more traditional basement areas for kitchens, for instance.

There could even be a second kitchen (sometimes called a still room) as well as separate spacious larders for dry stores, meat, game, milk and butter, plus storerooms or cleaning rooms for lamps and boots. All this means that a twentieth-century country-house servant's life might be a fraction easier, less smelly – even slightly healthier than it was in the previous century. Throw in the distant prospect of more privacy, like your own bedroom, if you eventually make it to the upper servant ranks, and though the incentive itself of more space may seem small to us, it still counts for something for the young and impoverished.

Food is another important reason why a country-house servant's job is desirable. Three – or even two – meals a day is unheard of in very poor homes, where a tiny amount of money has to stretch to several young hungry mouths. Meals in poverty-stricken homes are meagre, even sparse, mainly consisting of bread and jam or dripping, potatoes and a tiny amount of meat or fish, if they're lucky. As a servant, you get to eat regularly – one big main meal a day – and even though the food itself might consist of your employers' leftovers or badly prepared dishes, it is usually more substantial, with a bit more variety than at home. Think fairly bland nursery food, basic meat 'n' potatoes meals and you won't be far off. And the upper servants sometimes get a really good deal when it comes to food: much depends on how the house is run – and, of course, how considerate the employers are.

Finally, there's the proximity to wealth and influence, even if you are an 'invisible' helper, with gruelling working hours which start around 6am or earlier and often don't end until 10 or 11pm. No matter how strict the house rules are – country-house owners issue their own set of rules – and how mean-minded and spiteful the behaviour of your colleagues, being in a beautiful setting, around priceless possessions and sumptuous displays of wealth all the time or even, in a few cases, living in an up-to-date house where electricity, telephones and motorcars are already being used (though it's more likely to be a house where the old, less labour-saving ways are still in operation) is one more reason to understand why a life in country-house service is still regarded as a good option.

Though, of course, as part of all the rules and restrictions, even the upper servant will still have to address their employer as 'master' or 'mistress'. Wealthy house guests from across the Atlantic retain servants too – but they tell their hosts they never hear such servile phrases or terms from the mouths of their servants any more – in the US even servants are starting to be more upwardly mobile.

Yet the English servant, imbued with centuries of disciplined, subservient behaviour, discretion and an awesome level of deference to their betters, still, for now, remains a breed apart. Their expectations are so much lower.

Some interesting facts about the late nineteenth and early twentieth century:

THE WAY WE WERE...

- 1870: first water closet invented in England (a room with a flush toilet).
- 1876: invention of first telephone.
- 1896: Waddesdon Manor in Buckinghamshire, owned by the wealthy Rothschild family, is completed – with its own internal phone system comprising handsets (for the family) and earpieces (for the servants).
- 1900: the 17,000 acre estate at Welbeck Abbey, Nottinghamshire, owned by the Duke of Portland, employs 320 servants.
- 1900: 25 per cent of the population live in poverty; 10 per cent live below subsistence level and cannot afford an adequate diet. Many women can only feed the family by taking in washing or sewing at home – or pawning their own boots for food.
- 1900: average working week is 54 hours.
- 1901: census lists 100,000 servants whose ages are between 10 and 15.
- 1901: 2 million people work as domestic servants – 5 per cent of the total population.
- 1901: life expectancy for men: 45 years, for women: 49 years.

THE MARCH OF PROGRESS...

- 1902: Education Act raises school leaving age to 14.
- 1906: a Liberal Government is elected in a landslide victory after 10 years of Tory rule.

- 1907: free school meals are introduced for Britain's children.
- 1908: the first State pension: over 70s are entitled to a maximum of 5 shillings (25p) a week; Labour Exchanges are set up to help people find work.
- 1911: 48,000 drivers of motorcars or vans on the road.
- 1911: 2,000 cinema venues operating in Britain.
- 1918: Servants win the right to vote for the first time; women over 30 are also given the right to vote.

WHAT IT COST THEN – TYPICAL PRICES IN 1900:

- Pint of beer in a London public bar: 2d
- Pint of fresh milk: 2d
- Newspaper (*The Times*): 3d
- Inland letter postage: 1d

WAGES AND COST OF LIVING IN 1900:

- Manchester house servant: 18 pounds, 15 shillings a year
- Bank manager: £400 per annum
- 1903: Cost of brand new Napier seven-seater motorcar (Edwardian equivalent to a Rolls-Royce) is £520
- 1910: Average London property price is £14,000

A guest's chauffeur leaves
Welbeck Abbey in 1911.

Chapter 2

Money

There is an enormous disparity in the spending habits and incomes of the two classes. Financially, they inhabit different planets.

THE TOFFS: HOW TO SPEND IT

It starts from the top. In many ways, King Edward VII, Queen Victoria's son who takes the throne following her death in January 1901, is what we'd today probably call a 'king of bling', a party animal who loves to indulge himself with huge displays of extravagance and luxury.

In the long years before he is handed the regal crown, Edward, Prince of Wales, or 'Bertie', is a high-spending, gourmandizing, womanising king-in-waiting at the head of a 'smart set' of wealthy, highly influential socialites whose social calendar frequently revolves around following his lead. Their pursuits are many. And they usually involve huge expenditure:

shooting parties, balls, theatre trips, grand dinners with rich French cuisine, gambling sessions, cards, horse racing – if it's expensive and exclusive, they're doing it.

This is a highly social world. Yet to us it would seem incredibly public. With servants around all the time, taking care of your every need, how can it be otherwise? Yet despite this, within this set some are sexually promiscuous and unfaithful to their spouses – who might be aware of this but look away. Maintaining the status quo matters much more.

As King, Edward VII has half a million pounds a year (think around £8 million a year in today's money) in his pocket – and his coterie of super-rich friends and acquaintances, include many 'new' money millionaires and entrepreneurs whose fortunes frequently dwarf his own, as well as the fortunes of the 'old' money aristocrats.

Someone like the 6th Duke of Portland, William Cavendish-Bentinck (The King's Master of the Horse), for example, is much richer than his king. The Duke's vast estate, Welbeck Abbey in Nottinghamshire, plus his coal-mining interests, give him 'many millions per annum'.

So playing host to Edward and his chums for a big entertainment, a country-house weekend (called a 'Saturday to Monday' by the toffs because the expression 'weekend' is considered vulgar) or a shooting party, or a trip to the South of France, involves a fantastic amount of spending.

It's difficult to be a freeloader. Any player in this exclusive world is required to spend just as freely as the next person in their group when it's their turn – and the extravagances are huge. As King, Edward prefers the self-made entrepreneurs to the old-fashioned aristocrats, for the self-made 'showing off' – essentially for its own sake – is part and parcel of the super-toffs' way of life. Appearances count for everything.

Yet in some grand aristocratic houses, an announcement that

the King plans a visit can sometimes be greeted with consternation: so enormous is the cost of entertaining him and his cronies for just a few days it might involve a year's worth of economising for the host family – or even tip them into debt.

It isn't just the food and booze, the extravagantly displayed eight-course dinners of the finest French cuisine, the crates of the King's favourite French champagne, it's the little extras that pad out the bill: the finest cigars he loves to smoke, the heavy gambling sessions into the small hours, the lengthy shooting sessions of game. And, of course, there are the human 'extras' required for putting up the royal mistress of the time, in the regal style to which she is accustomed, naturally.

No detail is overlooked: this is a time when the status-conscious rich will go as far as to measure the height of their footmen – to make sure they're all the same height. After all, it won't look good to have two liveried footmen of different heights on either side of a door. Your friends might notice. And comment.

The King leads the way in this obsession with detail; at one point, he ticks off Consuelo, Duchess of Marlborough for having a semi-crescent of diamonds in her hair at dinner instead of a proper tiara. Shameful, eh?

At the other end of the scale, the working classes of the era frequently struggle to survive and feed large families on a standard wage of £1 a week or less. For the lower live-in servants, pay is sometimes much less than this. Yet the wealthy and slavish followers of the very latest fashion or trend don't blink an eyelid at forking out today's equivalent of £20–30,000 for a first-class return ticket, Southampton to New York, on one of the new transatlantic ocean liners going across the Atlantic to the New World.

At the brand new Ritz hotel in London, opening in 1906 to cater exclusively to the super-rich and their friends, fountains are created which spout only the finest champagne. Ultra-fashionable women think nothing of spending the equivalent of £3,000 on just one hat. It is standard practice to use their husbands' millions to visit Paris high fashion salons twice a year, ordering dozens of the most exquisite creations of the time from French designer houses like Worth or Doucet and having each dress shipped home, beautifully wrapped, in its own individual trunk (beats a cardboard Tiffany or Gucci box any day, doesn't it?).

Make no mistake, following on from the sober restraint of the Victorian years, this is a period of completely over-the-top conspicuous consumption for the wealthy. And the only ordinary people who really have a permanent close-up view of all this sumptuous extravagance are, of course, the servants – without TV and radio, many don't know much about the indulgences and excesses of the rich – though the newspapers of the time chronicle their travels – and their scandals, should they come to light.

Yet in some cases, things have been getting a bit tight financially for the aristocrats with the 'old' money. Not all estates are managed or run as well as they should be. Once they could do very nicely thank you by living off the agricultural proceeds of the estate. But not any more: many English aristocrats now find themselves in a situation where they might still be asset-rich in terms of jewels, shares and land, yet there's very little cash. So how do you find large sums of cash fast if you're juggling ever increasing debt, unwilling to sell off all or part of your huge estates? Where could you get money? Lots of it?

THE BIG TRADE-OFF: CLASS FOR CASH

Snobbery reigns supreme among the elite. By tradition, they only really want to stick to each other, and merge their aristocratic, high-born families through marriage to the offspring of other high-born toffs.

But money is money and while the aristocracy traditionally rely on primogeniture (the passing on of inheritance, land and title from father to eldest son) for hundreds of years, when pushed they have occasionally married for money outside the elite circle – provided the bride's dowry is tempting enough. When you've got a lot of money and can have whatever you want, why not aim higher?

But with the wind of change blowing through their lives and, in some cases, their fortunes dwindling through higher taxation or poor management, by the late nineteenth century many discover the need to find money to hang on to their estates is becoming quite urgent.

Borrowing more cash is no longer a good option. Until the late 1800s the aristocrats have always been able to borrow huge sums of money quite easily – at extremely favourable rates of interest. Those who chose this route and used the cash to improve their estates are now in trouble: their equity or land values have crashed with the big agricultural slump when food prices plummeted. Then, just like today, the days of cheap, easy borrowing dried up. Even for them. So the temptation to hold their noses and marry into the 'new' money families making vast fortunes in trade or industry is overwhelming. And this idea becomes even more compelling when they consider the incredible fortunes that have been made in recent years across the Atlantic Ocean.

Enter the super-wealthy American heiress. The cash-strapped British aristocratic snobs take one look at the enormous dowries of the daughters of families whose millions have been made in the railroads, shipping, land speculation, stock market and banking in America – and buy into the idea of a marriage with an American heiress.

In turn, the wealthy American mothers of beautiful young daughters are desperately keen to buy into the aristocracy – for them, a title and a grand country house in England is the stuff of dreams, the pinnacle of social achievement.

And the snobbish tendency of the 'old', inherited money looking down at 'new' money from trade or business has not been restricted to these shores. Through the second half of the nineteenth century, a handful of grand, wealthy New York families who live in snooty splendour on inherited money form a tight little 'upper' American clique, the country's social elite.

They're known as 'Mrs Astor's 400' – the number of wealthy people who can fit into the grand ballroom of the home of New York's most powerful socialite family, the Astors. The 400 have always been acutely disdainful of outsiders. They hate the idea of their children marrying those who made their fortunes from what they see as the 'vulgar' pursuits of trade or money-making. But that kind of snobbery is on the wane in America, too. Eventually they too give into the reality – there is far too much new money sloshing around to ignore it – and their children start to marry into it.

So by the late nineteenth and early twentieth century wealthy new-money Americans have become equally serious power players in this 'age of bling', spending millions on vast mansions, jewels and lavish entertaining – tens of thousands of dollars are blown on one outfit for a big New York costume party – in many ways aping the style and fashions of wealthy English aristocracy. But with one beady, lingering eye on the one status symbol their money cannot buy: class.

In the years between 1870 and 1914, hundreds of rich American girls are put on display before the English and European aristocrats by their pushy, socially ambitious mothers – hoping to propel them into what could be described as a carefully 'arranged' but very grand marriage, where the trade-off for their 'new' American cash is a title and a big country estate and a heritage going back centuries. Shedloads of it. An estimated 10 per cent of aristocratic marriages between 1870 and 1914 are with brides from the USA.

This 'Desperately Seeking An English Toff' system works in some cases. There's too much money involved for it not to work, and these girls have a wildly romantic notion about marrying an English earl or a duke. But there are huge cultural differences. As a result, some liaisons are unhappy, loveless and occasionally disastrous: wealthy, pampered American girls already used to servants and the latest mod cons like central heating complain endlessly about how chilly and cold the vast, unheated English mansions can be. The very English characteristic of 'putting up with it' or being stoic about physical inconvenience or discomfort has never really played well across the Atlantic. And there is a persistent belief among the English aristocracy, that lasts well into the twentieth century, that the only way to heat a room is by a fire – even though the cost of installing the 'new fangled' methods of heating their homes is affordable for some.

American social princesses arriving into the English or Scottish countryside are aghast to discover that every time they want a bath in their chilly new stately home, a housemaid has to lug gallons of water up and down stairs if the kitchen is tucked far away in a different part of the enormous house. And, if they are unlucky, their day-to-day relationship with their cash-strapped English aristocratic spouse, often overly concerned with the cares of keeping the estate running, can be as chilly or remote as the house itself.

In the *Downton Abbey* marriage, the Earl of Grantham believes he has secured the future of his estate this way by marrying the wealthy American heiress, Cora, Countess of Grantham. They wind up with three daughters and no male heir. Yet theirs is very much a love match rather than a mere merger of interests. Was this typical? Maybe not. Consider the story of the marriage of the fabulously rich railroad heiress Consuelo Vanderbilt and her marriage to 'Sunny', Charles Spencer Churchill, the ninth Duke of Marlborough and owner of the 187-room Blenheim Palace in Woodstock, Oxfordshire, in 1896.

THE GIRL WITH THE DIAMOND-ENCRUSTED GARTERS

Eighteen-year-old Consuelo's dowry (part of which was paid in railroad stocks and shares) is equivalent to US $100 million today. Newspaper stories at the time carry gushing reports about her bridal undies: her pink lace corset (with real gold hooks) and her silk stockings (held up by diamond-encrusted garters).

Yet Consuelo is a very unhappy bride. For starters, she's in love with someone else. However, so desperate is Consuelo's conniving mother Alva to up the ante socially by being mum to a duchess that Alva pretends to be dying in order to convince Consuelo to go through with the match.

Consuelo cries all the way to the glittering wedding ceremony. Some stories claim she's seen weeping at the altar. In their carriage afterwards, the Duke, close to bankruptcy, blithely informs her he's given up the woman he loves to marry her money. The honeymoon isn't even over when he orders a hugely expensive refurbishment of Blenheim.

Two sons are born. But the couple separate, a great society scandal in 1906 – even the King has insisted they should not divorce – and it isn't until 1921 that a divorce is finally granted.

So has the cash from the American heiresses 'saved' the British cash-poor, land-rich aristocracy from financial ruin? It certainly helped. Once you've sold off the family silver, your valuable art collection and other costly items to pay your debts the last thing you want to do is give up the house and the land.

THE WIND OF CHANGE

But the big social changes that are already starting to bubble underneath the surface in the Edwardian years – the rise of socialism, the suffragette movement with its push towards women's rights, and the growing political awareness of the needs of working people, pushed forward by the dawn of World War I – are far more significant in changing the entire landscape for the many, a tidal wave of change, if you like, than big windfalls of cash for the small but privileged minority.

And yet the innate snobbery of the aristocrats still prevails: many families still can't help looking down their noses on these rich, youthful, usually high-spirited American girls whose manners are perceived to be 'something between a Red Indian and a Gaiety Girl'.

In addition, the huge spending power of the American heiresses easily surpasses anything the British aristocrats have known. So there's an envy factor in there, too. The American girls are much better dressed, for starters. They think nothing of ordering 90 dresses at a time in Paris, only to wear them just once. (Wearing things once, of course, means no one can ever criticise you for donning the same garment again.)

By 1914, 60 peers of the realm and 40 sons of peers have married American women. So some of those balls, lavish parties, champagne-spouting fountains and the other many indulgences of the 'smart set' that followed Edward VII were indirectly underwritten by the millions flowing from the coffers of the American heiresses, as well as propping up the existence of some of the country's greatest estates.

In the time-honoured tradition of the 'if you've got it, flaunt it' set so follows the mantra: 'If you haven't got it any more, use other people's money'. After all, with so much hectic social networking at stake, who was going to let the outdated rules and snobbery of the older generation stop them?

Being Lady Bountiful

Yet despite all this big spending and trading of money for status, the mega-rich are not completely oblivious to the world beyond their own.

Outward appearances are everything. And while aristocratic families often treat their servants and those living on their estate as inferior beings from a separate planet, they are, at the same time, obliged to foster the general idea that they are moral guardians of the needy and less well off. They have to be seen to be conscious of their responsibilities to others. It is called *noblesse oblige*: if you are privileged and rich, you have a moral duty to public service and charity; it means you are seen to be putting your money to good use.

This idea – of patronising the poor with one hand, dispensing charity and goodwill from the Big House, and exploiting them with the other by using them as an astonishingly cheap labour force – promotes the centuries-old view of a paternalistic lord and master who is concerned about the wellbeing of his tenants. And in fairness, not all the big landowning families are cynical in their treatment of the poor people living on their estates; some genuinely do form good relationships with their tenants and want to help them.

Consuelo Vanderbilt, for instance, becomes well known for her devotion to the welfare of the poor people on the big Blenheim estate, and her concern for the wellbeing of her 40 live-in servants – a dedication to charitable works that manifests itself throughout her life. Yet the truth is, Consuelo is behaving according to all the rules and traditions that dictate the every move of a very wealthy aristocratic woman: the Edwardian mistress of a country estate is a key player in this demonstration of concern for the needy. It is her role and hers alone to be Lady Bountiful, dispensing goodwill locally, making visits and perhaps giving advice and hand-me-downs to the needy tenants.

Whatever her own feelings or views, the wealthy country-house wife is obliged, as an important duty, to visit the estate's tenants regularly, raise money for good causes like hospitals or for the sick and needy, and involve herself in fund-raising for local events such as bazaars, in garden parties and important dates on the estate social calendar. Many throw themselves into their charity work – it is, after all, the only route for independent initiative and action available to them. Everything else in their life is determined by a rigid series of rules and regulations – even their socialising and lavish entertaining follows a very specific set of rules.

They can't be housewives or mothers, even if they want to, because they have armies of servants to do all their work for them. Their family relationships, including those with their husbands, are all conducted in a rigid, pre-determined way. So while the Lady Bountiful role is a must for someone in this elevated social position – the other women in her social circle are usually equally involved in charitable works – it winds up serving a useful purpose: in the absence of a fully formed Welfare State, there is, at least, one resource for helping the poor.

Though both husband and wife have this duty to the community to fulfil, aristocratic men and their male heirs do not, as a rule, get very involved in the day-to-day detail of charity work. It's very much seen as women's territory. So in the midst of all the planning, running the household, socialising and emphasis on status, the mistress of the house must allocate time, in between shopping in Paris or organising (with a lot of help) extraordinarily extravagant, money-no-object dinners, to be a visible charitable presence.

Yet when you look at the tiny salaries the toffs are quite happy to pay their servants, you can only scratch your head and wonder about the hypocrisy of it all.

SERVANTS WAGES: SLAVE LABOUR?

Servants are always seriously underpaid and over-exploited. Over hundreds of years, the poorest people are expected to be grateful for food and shelter, in return for what is usually incessant, hard physical labour.

They accept that their masters and betters rule their lives, simply because there are no other avenues of work. If you are at the bottom of the heap, you either starve or get on with the job in hand. And if you are fortunate, you get an employer who treats you with a degree of consideration.

In previous centuries, some country-house owners regarded the servants as part of the family. But by the nineteenth century this idea had started to fade, though it did survive in a few estates.

THE WAGES OF SERVICE:

Until the nineteenth century, servants' wages were paid once a year. But gradually this changes, first to quarterly payments then, by the twentieth century, it becomes monthly. Men always earn more than women; usually, a woman receives half of a man's salary for an equivalent job. Depending on the post and the person's experience, the wages can increase – a little. However, a very young inexperienced person going into service for the first time might not receive any money at all initially: just food, a place to sleep and clothing.

Things are starting to improve a little for servants by the Edwardian era, because although there is still strong demand for their expertise, different types of work other than service have begun to emerge. Even working long, gruelling hours in a mill, a punishingly unhealthy way of making a living, may be seen as a better option: at least you have a semblance of freedom – you get to go home at the end of the day. Comparing that against a life in service where you get half a day off a week and are restricted in your behaviour by a series of inflexible rules (more about these in Chapter 4) – and where the penalty for breaking a rule can be instant dismissal – it's easy to see why even the nastiest of other working conditions are more appealing to many youngsters.

PERKS OF THE JOB

What sometimes makes country-house service a bit more attractive for some are the perks (perquisites), unofficial extras which come with the job. Here are a few examples:

Hand-me-downs

A lady's maid with a generous or kind mistress might be able to sell the odd item of clothing handed to her, if the maid has no use for it herself. Or she can use the material – always a really good quality fabric like wool, silk or cotton, man-made fabrics are never used – to make something else, perhaps a small dress for an impoverished young sister or relative. Good sewing skills are an important and valued attribute in a lady's maid.

Making deals

A butler or housekeeper might forge a relationship with

certain tradesman making regular deliveries to the house where they might agree a discount for continued orders. Or they might be able to sell any unwanted goods that are handed down from the household.

Tipping

This is another hidden extra in a world where there is much at-home entertaining of wealthy guests. Though it is primarily the personal servants like the butlers or valets who are more likely to be handed tips by a guest than, say, a housemaid.

Social Networking

Socially, since marriage means the end of working in service for women, a good looking young lady's maid hoping to find a husband views working in an elite household as a bit of a plus in the social stakes. There's more chance of meeting other male servants if you have a very social boss who moves around. And, of course, moving around means the chance to network and meet staff members from other households, also useful for those who hope to move from job to job.

Travel

While certainly a continuation of normal servant duties, without any real break in the non-stop, round-the-clock nature of their allotted role, travel gives a lady's maid, butler or valet the opportunity to broaden their horizons. The toffs are often on the move, travelling to other parts of the country for shooting parties, visiting their other homes (if they own several properties) and, of course, travelling abroad, sometimes within Europe (usually France or Italy), sometimes across the Atlantic to the US but also within the British Empire: a sea voyage to Africa, India or Australia is not unknown. And where the families also own town houses, the 'uppers' (meaning the servants with higher status) chance to socialise (on their half day off) is much greater in places like London, with its many entertainments, than it is in a more remote country area.

When the family do go away, it is customary to take just a few servants with them, leaving the rest of the staff in the country house. At such times, some families might give the remaining staff in the house cash as payment, in lieu of providing their meals. Other toffs stop providing any food at all while they're away – and just pay their servants' board wages.

WHEN EVERY PENNY COUNTS

Long-term upper servants can fare slightly better if their employer dies and the household is broken up. In some cases, they might receive a small gift as a legacy before they start to search for a new position. Or even a small pension.

Amazingly, given how tiny their pay packets are, many live-in servants do their best to save; when working really long hours (on average, 16–17 hours a day) with food and board provided, there is not much free time available to do anything but sleep. So it is not impossible to set aside a tiny sum of money.

The cash saved is frequently sent or handed out to support their own family, a household where there are often many very hungry mouths to feed. Even a very small amount of money from a very small pay packet can make a real difference to a family with one adult wage coming in.

Many poverty-stricken parents living in shockingly cramped and impoverished conditions actively welcome the idea of a teenage daughter going into service for this reason alone – and if she doesn't make the grade in service, there's no fulsome welcome home. Once you can earn, no matter how small a pittance your contribution, losing that meagre sum can put the survival of others on the line.

Long-term live-in servants also save whatever they can because they worry about their old age. State pensions do not exist until 1909 and, without savings, many servants face a very tough time indeed if they grow too feeble to work. There are country-house employers who treat their older servants kindly by giving them a small pension. But there are no guarantees of anything.

In the Edwardian era, London is the world's financial capital. In the years between 1890 and 1914, nearly half the international flow of capital is controlled by the City, or the Square Mile as we now know it. Millionaires from all over the world settle in London, buying grand houses in places like Park Lane or Grosvenor Square; they too become part of the wealthy coterie of Edward VII's smart set. Yet the servants they employ to do their bidding are, in many cases, virtual slaves, trapped by a rigid, harsh social hierarchy in a world where one false move or mistake can mean unemployment and ruin. The only way to survive is to work hard, focus on keeping the employer happy and accept the role you've landed; you could, after all, win a promotion in time. Even if you did, however, the roles of master and servant, as we will see, are very clearly defined...

THE HAVES

Churchill's American mother

One very successful early merger of American money and aristocratic class is the wedding of stunningly beautiful New York heiress Jennie Jerome to Lord Randolph Churchill, 2nd son of the Duke of Marlborough, in 1873. Their first-born son becomes British Prime Minister, Sir Winston Churchill.

Jennie's two sisters, Clara and Leonie, also marry into the English aristocracy, Leonie to one of the sons of Ireland's biggest landowning families; Clara marries an English aristocrat for love. Her husband, Morton Frewen, a financially incompetent son of English landed gentry has a nickname: 'mortal ruin'.

Throughout her twenty-year marriage to Lord Randolph, Jennie Churchill is reputed to have many lovers, young and old – among them King Edward VII – yet she becomes well respected and greatly admired as an unofficial 'ambassador' for American society in the influential, high-born circles of the time. Following Lord Randolph's death in 1895, she remarries – twice. She dies in 1921, following a fall down a flight of stairs – in a new pair of high-heeled shoes.

The status hunter's bible

Rich American mothers on the lookout for a titled spouse for their daughters subscribe to their own quarterly listings magazine called *Titled Americans: A list of American ladies who have married foreigners of rank*.

The magazine lists all the American women who have

already married aristocratic foreigners. And it carries a handy list of all the eligible titled bachelors, where they live, their incomes, the size of their estates and, in some cases, a listing of their debts.

The dancing marquess

Some of the cash-strapped British aristocrats of the time just blow their money for the hell of it. Take the antics of Henry Paget, the 5th Marquess of Anglesey, the 'dancing marquess'. On inheriting 30,000 acres in Staffordshire, Dorset, Anglesey and Derbyshire on the death of his father, plus an income of £110,000 a year – around £10 million in today's terms – Henry manages to blow the lot in six years.

Where does the money go? Lavish parties, yachts, extravagant theatrical productions – which frequently involve priceless costumes studded with expensive jewels – and Henry's own elaborate outfits. These include a diamond and sapphire tiara, a turquoise dog collar, ropes of pearls, and slippers studied with rubies. At one point he modifies his car so that the exhaust sprays out perfume. And it is rumoured that he likes to make his wife lie naked while he prances around, covering her body with jewels. Very soon he is mortgaging his estates to cover his mounting debts and, after finally being forced to sell off his jewels, dogs, cars and carriages he is declared bankrupt. He moves to the South of France, where he dies, age 30, in 1905.

The matchmaker

New York society snobs shun wealthy financier's daughter

Mary 'Minnie' Stevens because there is a rumour that she was once a chambermaid. But she still manages to up her social ante by marrying into the British aristocracy and becoming the wife of Sir Arthur Henry Fitzroy Paget. Once established as an aristocratic wife, she becomes a top-end marriage broker, introducing American heiresses to British aristocrats looking for wealthy brides. Yet the English toffs claim she has made society 'more shallow and vulgar' than before.

Send him the bill

Because male and female roles in the aristos' world are so rigidly cast, paying the bills is always the man's responsibility. The mistress of the house never carries any money at all. An English aristocratic wife is never involved in the financial planning of their estates. Yet she can spend – things like expensive clothing and décor are considered part and parcel of the massive effort in maintaining appearances at all times, and, of course, keeping up with the other wealthy women in their set.

THE HAVE NOTS

What servants earn in 1910:
- The Butler: £50–£100 a year
- The Housekeeper: £40–£70 a year
- The Cook or Chef: £18–£500 a year
- The Valet: £35–£50 a year
- Lady's Maid: £20–£32 a year
- First Footman: £30–£40 a year
- Second Footman: £20–£30 a year

- First Housemaid: £28–£30 a year
- Second Housemaid: £22–£24 a year
- Kitchen Maid: £20–£24 a year
- Scullery Maid: £10–£14 a year
- Chauffeur: £10–£25 a year
- Hallboy: £16–£18 a year
- Nanny: £30–£40 a year
- Governess: £22–£40 a year

Chapter 3

The Pecking Order

Everyone living in or around the grand country estate has a set role to play in the hierarchy of the house. And this strict adherence to the pecking order, the set tasks or duties allotted to each person, isn't merely a template for the servants.

Even the owners of the estate, the master and mistress of the house, are locked into rigid, firmly set behaviour patterns, a 'job description' if you like, of how they must conform to what society expects of them. The pecking order runs from the very top of the tree to the lowliest person in the house. 'Everyone in their place' describes it perfectly.

THE FATHER
The father of the aristocratic family heads up the whole enterprise. He's the indisputable lord and master of the household. In Edwardian Britain, rich or poor, the family is the

most important aspect of everyday life – so the father, or man of the house, is always very much the focal point.

The father's authority is absolute: family members, whatever their feelings, cannot challenge or question his authority. He makes the decisions on everything: money, the estate, their social circle, the children's education, the family's religious and political affiliations and the path any sons and heirs might pursue, such as politics. (Daughters are only expected to marry someone equally grand and wealthy.)

No matter how rich they are or how ancient the family lineage, it is the patriarch of the grand country estate who controls the purse strings – and the family's fortunes. Certainly, he will give out the rewards and the praise to his offspring. But he can also be the one to dish out the punishment. So the penalties for stepping out of line or disagreeing with him are harsh: adult children who fail to obey his wishes risk being 'cut off' financially or, in some cases, being packed off out of sight to a foreign country. (Since only the toffs and the wealthy middle classes travel at these times, such banishment abroad is not some kind of treat as we might see it – it means 'get out of my sight'.)

Yet the wealthier the family and the bigger the estate, the bigger the headache when it comes to running the family fortunes. Inheritance, of course, is always a major problem for aristocrats without a male heir. But even in families with one or more sons and daughters, there needs to be sufficient cash in the kitty to provide a good cash legacy for all the children and dowries for the girls when they marry. And if they don't marry, there still needs to be a legacy. So this close eye on the financial affairs and the running of the estate is the aristocratic father's preoccupation: with thousands of acres and hundreds of rooms to consider, let alone a payroll of many servants, indoor and out, it's a huge responsibility.

JACKY HYAMS

He has a battalion of people to help him with this, of course: an estate manager or steward (an educated person with financial skills who lives, with his family, on the estate) plus city-based solicitors and accountants with whom he corresponds or visits regularly. This all takes up a considerable amount of time, particularly if there is more than one estate to run. But this not his only big responsibility. He may sit in the House of Lords, for instance (by tradition, he's a Conservative). And, of course, his neighbourhood duties, also by tradition, may involve acting locally as a Justice of the Peace or a Lord Lieutenant.

All of this means that as a father he can be a very distant authority figure, a hands-off dad, especially in the case of his daughters; sons are much more important because they are seen as the future of the family's wealth and prestige.

Essentially, the army of servants, the nannies, the governesses and the nurses are the ones whose lives revolve around the daily aspects of parenting. He's far too busy with his important duties to spend time just being a dad…

THE MOTHER

Wives, in Edwardian times, are supposed to behave as obedient and compliant partners; equality in marriage doesn't come into it. The aristocratic wife has a major role to play in the organisation of how the house is run, yet she is far too busy with her many and varied duties to have anything like what we'd recognise as a normal relationship with her children. Or her husband, come to that.

There is an allotted time each day to see her children – usually around tea time, for about an hour, and that's it, though in some exceptions she could find more time for them during the day.

She has so many time-consuming functions, the first being to oversee and liaise with the upper servants – particularly the cook and the housekeeper – on the day-to-day running of the house. There will frequently be large numbers of people to entertain in the house, sometimes for several days at a time. So the organisation and forward planning of all this requires a lot of attention to detail.

Then there is the house itself, its décor and appearance. Overall responsibility for this is a crucial aspect of her role at all times; her husband won't concern himself with any of this. Yet it is highly important: the family are judged and evaluated by the appearance of the house, the servants and its interior. If the curtains are tatty, it reflects on the entire family. If she notices that a servant looks less than clean, neat and tidy, a comment to the housekeeper can mean admonishment – or even the sack –for the girl. She has to be constantly alert to all the finer details. Yes, there is an army of servants to polish, clean, produce meals and ease the path at all times, but being bang up to date on the latest interior innovations is a must: as style and fashion conscious as she has to be when it comes to what she wears, so it follows that the home has to have the right 'look'.

As well as her duties as a local Lady Bountiful, she is also, in some cases, a political hostess. So her judgements when entertaining the high and the mighty need to be fine-tuned; she needs to be up to date regarding what's going on in the social world around her, though it's not acceptable yet for aristocratic women to 'meddle' in politics. Her allies in this need for information might be relatives, particularly unmarried aunts or cousins, who can usually be relied upon to trade gossip when they're visiting. Or she writes to them regularly, as well as corresponding with the other aristocratic wives in her circle: this kind of networking is also particularly useful when it comes to hiring new servants.

So there it is – a highly decorative hostess, interior decorator, Lady Bountiful dispensing charity to the poor and big-budget party planner. Throw in the travelling and the unending social pressure to behave in a certain way at all times and you can see that behind all the luxury and show, this is a complex role. And there is little real privacy. With so many people around at her beck and call, even her private life can be subject to intense scrutiny. Which might not be a problem if, like Cora, Duchess of Grantham, her marriage is a happy one, a fact well known and discussed below stairs. But if, like some aristocratic wives, her relationship with her husband is a starchy, formal affair, a merger purely for financial or status reasons and very 'hands off', (there's no divorce, of which more later), rather than envy her elevated role you might wonder how she copes with it all.

THE SERVANT ROLES

Each individual job in the pecking order is very clearly set out and compartmentalised. This way, the lower servants can hone their skills over time. Essentially, the older staff teach the younger ones – who have the most harsh, menial and unrelenting workload. In fact, the learning curve means the younger lower servants sometimes have to wait on their senior co-workers. It also means they can pick up the nuances of the household itself. They may not have face-to-face contact with the people they work for, but they still need to be familiar with their whims and fancies.

Not everyone who goes into country house service sees it as 'a job for life'. Here are the four different types:

- The servant who spends their entire life in service.
- The servant who wants the country-house lifestyle and regards it as a stage before marrying (on average, women in

service marry at around the age of 25, and have worked for around l2 years in 3–5 different jobs).

- The impoverished, genteel, educated woman (think Jane Eyre), usually a governess or housekeeper, forced to find paid work because of a change of circumstance in her family's fortunes.
- The local 'casual' worker or labourer.

THE UPPER SERVANTS

THE BUTLER

The butler is the highest-ranking servant in the house. He has total responsibility for all the male staff in the house and is, effectively the 'team leader' of the servants – and the right-hand man of his master. He is respectful – but never subservient.

He's in charge of the wine cellar, the arrangement of the dining table, the announcement of dinner and, with the footmen, the serving of all meals and wine. It is the butler's job to carve the joint of meat and remove the silver covers from the dishes. It is also his job to check that lamps or candles are in working order and that the fires are glowing. At the day's end he is the person who checks that all doors and windows in the house are locked.

He is responsible for all the family silver and all the arrangements for the reception of guests. Immaculate in appearance, discreet in the extreme, he is superbly well organised; his key priority in life is his boss and the family.

He is on call 24/7 and is the person who has most to do with the people 'upstairs'. Usually a bachelor (his bosses prefer him not to be distracted by a life of his own), he has worked his way up the servant hierarchy over time, so the butler's knowledgeable authority over his male underlings is never questioned.

He has his own suite of rooms, usually as near to the main living rooms, usually the dining room, as is practical. Being so close means that whenever he is summoned by a bell, he can reach his employer's side as quickly as possible. His suite of rooms also includes a dining area for the upper servants, a butler's pantry, where the silver plate is washed and polished and, nearby, a silver vault which stores the valuables; only the butler is permitted to have the key to this.

He is the ultimate 'front of house' man. He opens the front door to visitors – or accepts a calling card if the family is not available. If the family has a phone, he takes the phone calls and messages. Within his suite he also has an office where he interviews prospective employees, draws up timetables for male staff, works out the duties of the day for the footmen, pores over the seating plans for lunch and dinner and coordinates the plans for big social events like the weekend shooting parties.

His cellar duties include storing the wine bottles in their correct place, stocking up on the wines, champagne, port, sherry, brandy and liqueurs – and consulting with the master on which wines are to be served at mealtimes. (He might also be allowed to sell off the empty wine bottles as a little perk of the job.)

His manners must be impeccable at all times. He needs to know every single like and dislike of his employer – and those of the many guests. If his employer insists on having his newspapers perfectly flat before reading, it is the butler who instructs the footman to toast and iron them in readiness for the breakfast table. If he hands a guest a drink, it must be their preferred tipple – they do not need to ask. His calm demeanour and attention to detail are second to none: like everything else in the house, his comportment is a reflection of his employer's status. Everything must be perfectly organised – right down to the last detail.

THE HOUSEKEEPER

Next in rank to the butler, the housekeeper is the most senior female servant and effectively the second-in-command, the other essential link in the chain making up a well-run household.

In her stiff black dress, silk apron trimmed with beads, lace collar, small lace cap and belt jingling with keys (everything she is held accountable for, from spices to china and linen, must be locked up) she has a lot of responsibility. Though she must defer to the butler at all times.

Her duties include the supervising, engaging and dismissing of female staff (with the exception of the nanny, lady's maid and cook who are hired personally by the mistress of the house). The discipline and behaviour of the female staff is part of the housekeeper's remit.

She is called 'Mrs' even though she is usually unmarried, because the rank of a married woman is more important. She needs a good head for figures because her role involves keeping the accounts of the household expenditure, writing down all sums of money paid out, ordering goods from the tradesmen – perhaps getting a discount or 'commission' from regular suppliers – and, with the approval of her mistress, paying their bills as well as the accounts for all the other expenses of the house.

It is the housekeeper's role to allocate all the duties to be carried out by the female staff – and to make sure that all the tasks, the cleaning, dusting and polishing of all the rooms, are carried out properly. She keeps a detailed inventory and ensures that both family and staff have a clean supply of linen and bedding. All the household necessities, things like soap, sugar, flour, spices and candles, must be accounted for in her paperwork. This, of course, is carefully checked with the mistress of the house on a regular basis.

The housekeeper's quarters include a comfortable and well-furnished sitting room, where the lower servants sometimes wait on her. She has a bell pull which connects with one of the many bells located in the corridor outside to summon staff to her room. Her quarters are also used as a housekeeping storeroom, with huge tall cabinets containing the very finest china and porcelain. She's responsible for checking all the washing and drying of the china following mealtimes: she must be on the lookout for any cracks or breakages. And she oversees and supervises everything in the still room – a place often used for making jams, homemade wines and distilled waters.

She also has her own medicine cabinet for the servants, which contains a number of herbal remedies and ointments to ease aches and pains.

The sitting room also has a large desk and this is where the housekeeper checks the accounts and does all her paperwork. Each day, she must meet with the mistress of the house to get her instructions and discuss all the items of expenditure.

If there are visitors due to stay, she will ensure that all the details are in order so that the smooth running of the house and comfort of the guests is not affected by the extra work such entertaining entails.

As a supervisor, she is not expected to do any rough, menial tasks. As long as her absence doesn't create any problems in the way the house operates, she can arrange her own time off. If the family are away, visiting relatives or travelling, together with the butler and lady's maid, she is in charge of the house in their absence – and has to make sure everything is ready for their return.

THE COOK

The cook of the house runs her own domain below stairs – and her status, in the wealthiest homes, is high: she has staff to carry out many tasks, kitchen and scullery maids at her behest: a senior kitchen maid, for instance, may be under Cook's instructions to prepare the meals for the other servants while the cook occupies herself with the needs of the family. And under Cook's rule, none of the other servants may enter the kitchen other than the kitchen staff.

Cook's ingredients are prepared for her by the kitchen staff and the scullery maids are responsible for the cleanliness of the food preparation area. The cook is also responsible for the dining room and the areas around the kitchen.

She starts work at 6am and usually finishes around 10pm or later. Once dinner has been served at night, most of her day's duties are over because the cleaning up chores are the remit of her kitchen staff (painfully labour-intensive work in a world without dishwashers when you consider that when guests were visiting, dinner for eighteen people might mean over 500 separate items of fine china, silver and valuable glassware and cutlery had to be cleaned).

She too has her own room and her main responsibility each morning is to meet with the mistress of the house to check and approve menus; often, a basic knowledge of French is required as the wealthy Edwardians love to gorge on French food when entertaining. (French male chefs were very much in vogue among the very wealthiest families wanting to impress their guests. But such chefs could be both temperamental and expensive: a top female country house cook would earn an average of £30–£60 a year, yet a top French chef could command as much as £500 a year.)

After the morning meeting with her mistress, the cook prepares soup for the next day. (The Edwardians prefer to drink soup the day after it is made.) Then she sets about creating the pastries, jellies, creams and entrées needed for the evening meal; then it's time to supervise the family's lunch. After that, if she's lucky, there's a brief lull in kitchen proceedings until the whole thing revs up again for that night's dinner.

With one half day off a week (usually Sunday) and elaborate meals consisting of several courses, the cook's world is hectic, hot, pressurised and unrelenting: everything has to be prepared and presented to perfection (the presentation of the food on display is just as important as the taste), so there is no room for cock-ups. Usually, she's suspicious of change and any 'new fangled' devices in the kitchen – Cook likes things run her way and her way alone. With so much perfection at stake, can you blame her?

THE VALET

The valet is, like the lady's maid, a personal servant, dedicated entirely to the personal appearance of his master. He waits on him when his master is dressing and undressing, brushing his master's hair, cutting it if necessary and shaving him, too. He folds up all his master's clothes, brushes them and lays them out in readiness for him to wear, according to custom and time of day, after making sure they have been suitably aired before wearing. (Since both aristocratic men and women change clothes frequently throughout the course of the day, his duties are as onerous as any other servant, especially when guests are in the house and the activities of the day involve outdoor pursuits.)

It is the valet's responsibility to look after all clothing or footwear repairs if needed and to put the clothes away in the appropriate fitted cupboards or wardrobes.

His master's clothes are always protected from dust or dirt with brown Holland (a heavy, plain linen unbleached cloth, also used for blinds) and other linen wrappers. On sunny days, wardrobes are left wide open in order to air them. One wardrobe contains just shirts and underclothes, other cupboards contain different types of outdoor clothing: some aristocrats might have more than 60 suits to be looked after so there is always plenty of room to store the clothes. Expensive silk pyjamas, often embroidered with the family crest, are perfectly folded and kept in a tallboy with several drawers. (The valet also needs to be an expert packer and folder of clothes; everything must be folded in perfect symmetry.)

The valet checks his master's boots and shoes (usually cleaned by an under footman) before setting them out in the dressing room. While a housemaid cleans the grate, lights the fire and sweeps and dusts the room, the valet is busy preparing the washing-table, arranging the shaving apparatus, running his master's bath (if the house is not plumbed for hot running water, a lower servant will bring up the hot water required for washing).

Then, after his boss has gone down to breakfast, he dries the razor, washes any hairbrushes or combs thoroughly in warm water, and empties and dries the hand basin. Because of the personal nature of his work, he sometimes has quite a close relationship with his boss. One rung above the head footman, one rung below the butler, he may well be a recipient of his master's confidences; John Bates (played by Brendan Coyle in *Downton Abbey*) who had previously worked as the Earl of Grantham's batman during the Boer War, is typical of a reliable valet's diligence and loyalty, acquired over years of working his way up the servant hierarchy.

THE LADY'S MAID

The lady's maid is directly hired by the mistress of the house, and reports to her rather than the housekeeper. As a result, her position with the rest of the staff is somewhat tricky; many of the lower servants dislike her and worry that she will snoop around and tell tales on them. This can sometimes make her feel a bit isolated, and although she has some privileges the lowers never enjoy, at the end of the day she is very much a servant.

As a dresser, escort to her mistress and personal servant, a lady's maid needs many skills, particularly sewing, because she is responsible for all the care of her mistress's clothing, including all repairs of garments and hats; she can even be a substitute for the dressmaker or local seamstress at times. She also, like the valet, needs to be an expert packer because she accompanies her mistress on her travels.

A lady's maid also needs to be able to read and write well, be very neat and clean in appearance, cheerful and pleasant in demeanour and, above all, honest: she has to handle and take care of all her mistress's expensive clothes, her jewel box and many other valuable items. Like the butler and valet, she needs to be discreet about what she hears and sees around her. If she does indulge in gossip with the other servants about anything (and the temptation to do this is strong) she faces losing her job without any hope of a 'character', the reference required to move on to another job, if her disloyalty reaches the ears of her boss.

Though her career prospects are not very good because she doesn't have the necessary kitchen experience to help her rise up to the role of housekeeper, she has her own room, usually cleaned for her by one of the lower housemaids, who also wakes her each day with a cuppa. She is allowed to bathe regularly in the female upper servants' bathroom and, because she does not have to wear the pinafore assigned to those whose work is menial, she is often quite well dressed: her mistress's expensive hand-me-downs are frequently given to her to use as she wishes. She is also expected to be knowledgeable about beauty aids and potions – and how to look after and clean her mistress's expensive jewellery, the pearl necklaces and diamond earrings, heirlooms handed down through the generations.

Her working day starts by waking her mistress with tea and toast. Then they discuss the day ahead and the clothes her mistress wants to wear. Then she draws her mistress's bath, lays out the clothes, including the underwear, and, once her mistress has washed, she helps her to dress. Given the amount of hooks on the corsets and dresses the wealthy women wear at the time, it is virtually impossible to get dressed without some help. Corsets have to be laced tightly, silk stockings rolled onto the feet and up the legs and corset suspenders fastened; the whole painstaking and slow process of dressing and undressing – sometimes several times a day – is one of the lady's maids more repetitive tasks.

Once her mistress is seated at her dressing table – covered with beautiful and expensive silver brushes, large bottles of expensive French perfume and other costly toiletries – the lady's maid tends to her mistress's hair, brushing it and then piling it up into the elaborate upswept style of the day. Washing and dressing her mistress's hair with combs and tiaras is another big part of the job. Her mistress's hair is always long and piled high: loose hair is only for the boudoir.

As the mistress goes off to breakfast, the lady's maid tidies up, collects dirty garments for washing, checks for any clothing that needs brushing or sponging. Then she goes back to her own room where she spends time sewing, mending or washing items like corsets or silk stockings. She often uses a sewing machine – introduced in the 1850s – and the alterations she makes, adding trims to garments, adding feathers to hats, often take up a lot of time. There's also a great deal of ironing of the beautiful silks, chiffons, cotton and linen clothing her mistress wears. Then, summoned by a bell, she is back at her mistress's side to help her change her clothes again, if the mistress is planning a visit or a riding session. Even the corset might also have to be changed again to suit the outfit. And hair might have to be redone, too.

It's a non-stop job: when her mistress goes out, the lady's

maid accompanies her, helping her in and out of the carriage (or the car) arranging or removing her outerwear as needed, attending to her needs while she's away from home. Later, she will be helping her mistress change and dress for dinner, then she must wait until her mistress is ready to retire, helping her undress, plaiting her hair, (a common custom in Edwardian times) and helping her to bed.

If there are guests, the lady's maid will usually have spent the hours before she is summoned to help her mistress retire, sewing in her room, sometimes in the company of the other housemaids. Sometimes she doesn't get to bed until midnight. She has the satisfaction of knowing that her mistress will sometimes confide in her, even ask her advice. But whatever the confidences, she can never make suggestions or offer her own ideas unless asked. She is treading a fine line; she cannot, for one minute, forget that she is only a servant.

NURSERY STAFF: THE GOVERNESS OR THE TUTOR

These roles are very much about the care and education of the children in the family, so these people are, to an extent, less involved with the other staff. But the governess or tutor, because they are educators, are upper servants, often from better backgrounds than the lowers, perhaps coming from families of impoverished clergy or respectable traders that have fallen on hard times.

They are just as snobbish about their status as their employers. As a result, the governess is often resented by the lower staff, who dislike her airs and graces. Frequently they are required to travel with their bosses if the entire family goes abroad or visits relatives in the country. They never venture into the servants' hall, where the lowers eat and socialise. Depending on the employer, they may be invited to dine with the family.

The big nursery area itself is very much a separate world

in another part of the big house. Depending on the number of children in the house, any number of servants may be employed there.

If there are two small children in the house, for instance, this will usually involve a staff of four servants to look after them: a nanny and under nurse, a nursery maid and another maid to wait on them all. Their living/working quarters may consist of a day nursery, a night nursery, a lavatory, a room for the nanny (which she might be required to share with one other servant) and a small kitchen.

In the evening, the governess, like her employer, always changes clothes for dinner – if there are guests for this occasion this could mean evening dress – and if not dining with the family, she eats with the uppers. The nanny and other nursery staff do not mix with the other servants: they eat all their meals in the nursery. And they only speak to the downstairs servants if they run into them. Which isn't very often.

THE CHAUFFEUR

The role of the chauffeur is new in the Edwardian era. Effectively, he replaces the coachman and what he can earn varies considerably; if he already has experience as a chauffeur with another big household, he can command more.

Like the governess, the chauffeur is often resented by certain other staff: people working in the stables, for instance, resent the idea of the 'new fangled' motorcar and the huge changes it ushers in. But he is a member of the household, nonetheless, usually with his own room – though sometimes he might have a cottage on the estate – and a schedule which means being available at all times to transport the family wherever they wish and maintaining the upkeep of the car, getting spare parts if needed; he must also ensure there's enough petrol to drive the family around. He usually reports to the butler.

The Lower Servants

THE FOOTMAN

A successful footman can, with hard work, jump rank to a valeting or even a butler's role, which is why Thomas (Rob James-Collier), the scheming first footman in *Downton Abbey*, reacts with anger when he doesn't get the promotion to valet he'd hoped for.

Footmen have many duties and work long hours upstairs and downstairs, yet theirs is also an ornamental role: there's a lot of standing around, looking good. Height is very important. A footman over five-foot, ten-inches can command more money than a shorter man of that rank.

Their uniforms, white tie, starched shirt front and tails with brass buttons, sometimes stamped with a family crest, are provided by their employer – unlike the maids who must pay for their own uniform. They may work as a team of three, (ranked First, Second and Third Footman, all in order of status) on a rota system, 'close waiting' (looking after family members) on one day, the next day 'waiting' (household duties) and a third day 'carriage (or motorcar) waiting' (out and about with the family).

Upstairs, they serve at table, announce visitors, assist the guests in their rooms, attend the gentlemen in the smoking room after dinner and work in the front hall as the dinner guests are leaving, helping them with their clothing and into their carriages.

Downstairs they look after all the silver, glass and china, polish all the mirrors and the silver plate, dust in high places, clean the downstairs furniture and outdoor clothing – including the muddy riding boots and walking shoes – even ironing the master's newspaper (with a petrol-driven iron) to fix the ink. (Ironing newspapers is a fairly common duty because the toffs like everything to be flat as well as neat.)

The footman carries coal upstairs for the fires and lugs blocks of ice into the area where these are stored. In a country house where electricity has not yet been installed, they have the unenviable task of cleaning all the lamps, polishing the brass, de-griming the brass chimney, trimming the wicks, changing the oil regularly and checking, each night, that the lamps have gone out.

Footmen are exposed to guests and other people constantly, so they are expected to be the most presentable of all the servants; a good-looking, six-foot footman brings a touch of glamour to the proceedings. And although the days of highly costumed footmen, in powdered wigs and bright livery, are on the wane by the early 1900s, there are occasions when they may be required to don livery provided by their employers. They have more visibility than many of the other lowers, whose presence and work goes on unseen by those above stairs. As a consequence, they are often disliked within the servant hierarchy for giving themselves 'airs above their station'.

Yet no matter how they are viewed, footmen are constantly on the go from dawn to dusk, sleep in shared accommodation, and the work itself is monotonous and exacting to the last detail: a footman must wear special white gloves so as not to mark the silver when he is laying the table.

THE HOUSEMAID

It's a toss-up between the housemaid and the scullery maid as to who has the worst deal: they both have a backbreaking, labour-intensive role to play – housemaids do nothing but clean, sweep, dust, make beds, polish, lug pails of water and generally do whatever the housekeeper orders, though there is usually a head housemaid to supervise them in a large household employing several of these servants.

As a group, housemaids are very much regarded collectively

rather than as individuals: they must walk about the house together, in single file. Or sit together in the servants' hall in the brief gaps between their duties, sewing.

Each housemaid is allocated a set number of responsibilities, starting work at between 5.30 and 6am. Their first task is to make tea for the lady's maid and housekeeper and by 6.30am they are busy lighting fires, cleaning all the public rooms of the house, making beds, sweeping, dusting and cleaning the bedrooms, the bathrooms and the other rooms, scrubbing floors, sweeping ashes, polishing grates, windows and ledges, cleaning the marble floors and all the furniture, brushing carpets, beating rugs, carrying coal to the fireplaces and making sure the fires are stoked properly.

In some cases, one housemaid works only for the upper staff, another is allocated a specific room to clean all the time. Because there's great emphasis on specific rooms for specific purposes, a housemaid can be allocated a medal room, with rows of steel cases containing medals – which must be polished (with emery paper) every single day. Or when there's a house party, it's often the housemaid who has to wash the loose change the men in the party have emptied from their pockets and left out the previous night, so that a valet may return the shining coins to their owners later on.

A very hard-working housemaid can work her way up to a housekeeper's role. If she can handle the relentless monotony – and the sheer physical slog of doing nothing but clean for 14–16 hours a day.

THE SCULLERY MAID

The scullery maid is consigned to the kitchen only, the lowest-ranking female servant below the kitchen maids and the cook.

Her day begins around 4am because she must clean the grates and lay out the fire to heat the water if the cooking is being done on a coal-fired range. She must also dust the kitchen and scullery area before Cook starts work. Then it's back to the kitchen, for an endless round of washing up all the pots, pans, dishes, plates and cutlery for all the meals of the day. In between washing-up she must set the table for the servants' meals, wash the vegetables, peel potatoes, rub blocks of cooking salt through a sieve – and constantly make sure the big area in and around the kitchen is as clean as possible. The washing-up is endless – each copper pan used for cooking has to be thoroughly cleaned after use with a mixture of sand, salt, flour and vinegar.

Ignored by the household, often ridiculed by the upper servants and at the very bottom of the pecking order, the scullery maid has a very raw deal indeed. As raw as the skin on her hands.

PUG'S PARLOUR

The lower servants deeply resent the uppers and the marked distinction in their status. So they have a nickname for them. They call them 'Pugs' (in honour of the upturned nose and downturned mouth of the pug dog, so popular at the time). So the housekeeper's sitting room, her powerbase, is dubbed 'The Pug's Parlour' – because after meals, the uppers follow each other, in strict order of rank, down the corridor into the housekeeper's room to eat the final course of pudding or cheese.

WHAT'S IN A NAME?

Although the butler is always addressed by the family by his surname – Mr Carson in *Downton Abbey* – the toffs always address their footmen by their first names. Yet the names they use are unlikely to be their footmen's real names. The names Charles, John or James are used to address these servants, regardless of how they were christened. Better than 'hey you'. But another way of reminding them that they are mere underlings.

NO CHANCE OF A CUDDLE, THEN?

The toffs insist on segregating the sexes of their servants at all times, even when daily cleaning duties are involved. For instance, a housemaid allocated a specific bedroom to clean must attend to the fireplaces, windows and ledges, sweep the floors and the carpets – and then wait for the dust to settle. Only then can she leave the room. And only then can the footman come in to do his job of polishing the furniture. They are not allowed to be cleaning the same room together – especially a bedroom!

THE LIVE-IN LAUNDRY

By 1911 laundry maids are on the decline because some families now send all laundry out to big commercial laundries. (Some country families send their laundry off to a preferred top people's laundry in London, because it can be dispatched and returned by rail.) But other country-house owners more resistant to change prefer to continue to launder at home, some with a new, slightly different system: replacing the old in-house laundry with one attached to a small four-bedroom cottage some distance away from the house on the estate.

The cottage laundry uses traditional laundry methods – there's still no electricity – and three or four laundry maids live in the cottage, earning £1 a week in board wages, which goes into a kitty and is given to the head laundress, who shares the profit among the girls. Long hours and a hard slog for them – but a slightly more flexible system. And a fraction more independence.

THE BELLS, THE BELLS

The system of summoning servants by wire bell-pull systems installed in the house was originally established in the eighteenth century. Yet many aristocratic households were still using the bell system well into the twentieth century.

A housemaid
circa 1900.

Chapter 4

The Rules

'The Rules' involve everyone working in the big country house. And they cover virtually everything to do with daily life – communication, cleaning, eating and drinking; only sleeping is a rule-free zone – and for the servants, there's precious little of that, anyway. Rules vary from house to house, but they are very much fixed conditions of service and there isn't much flexibility.

Family members, of course, have different rules involving their own world – but they also have a specific set of rules around their treatment of their servants.

Here's a summary of the kind of rules they were expected to follow:

THE MASTER-SERVANT RELATIONSHIP RULES
- All family members must maintain appropriate relationships with the staff. As upper servants work directly

to the family, a trusting and respectful relationship should be established.

- Footmen are a proclamation of wealth and prestige. They are representatives of the household and family and, as such, it is advantageous that a good relationship is developed. However, as lower servants they do not expect to be addressed outside the receipt of instructions.

- While the housemaids will clean the house during the day, they should make every care and attention never to be observed doing their duties. If, by chance they do meet their employer, they 'give way' to the employer by standing still and averting their gaze, whilst the employer walks past, leaving them unnoticed. By not acknowledging them, the employer spares them the shame of explaining their presence.

- The mode of address to the staff has to be correct and proper. There is no 'Hey, you' or 'Excuse me'. It has to be precisely the right title, according to the status of the servant. Or, in some cases, nothing at all because the employer does not wish, at any time, to be reminded of the physical presence of the lower servants.

How to address a servant

- The Butler should be addressed courteously by his surname.
- The Housekeeper should be given the title of 'Mrs' (or Missus).
- The Chef de Cuisine should be addressed as such – or by the title 'Monsieur'.
- The Lady's Maid should be given the title of 'Miss' regardless of whether she is single or married. It is acceptable for the Mistress to address her by her Christian name.

- A Tutor should be addressed by the title of 'Mister'.
- A Governess should be addressed by the title of 'Miss'.
- It is the custom in old houses that, when entering into new service, lower servants adopt new names given them by their masters. With this tradition certain members of staff are renamed. Common names for matching footmen are James and John. Emma is popular for housemaids.
- It is not expected that the employer takes the trouble to remember the names of all staff. Indeed, to avoid conversation with them, lower servants will endeavour to make themselves invisible. As such, they should not be acknowledged.

SERVANT RULES

Written rules for the servants are equally draconian. Each country house has their own set of written rules for the servants, organised by the butler and housekeeper. Curiously enough, while the penalties for breaking these rules are often harsh, there are times when the master or mistress of the house might be a tad more sympathetic or forgiving of a breach of the rules than the butler and/or housekeeper. This is probably because they've slogged their way up the servant hierarchy over a period of many years and stick to the old 'I came up the hard way, so must you' maxim, while the employer, waited on at all times, has no real sense of the reality of the servant's lot and can, depending on their personality, give in to a kinder, more sympathetic gesture.

Here's a sample of Servant Rules (taken from the archives of Hinchingbrooke House, a country house in Cambridgeshire):

- Your voice must never be heard by the ladies and gentlemen of the household, unless they have spoken directly to you a question or statement which requires a response. At which time, speak as little as possible.

- Always 'give room' that is, if you encounter one of your employers in the house or betters on the stairs you are to make yourself as invisible as possible, turning yourself toward the wall and averting your eyes.
- When being spoken to, stand still, keeping your hands quiet. And always look at the person speaking to you.
- Never begin to talk to ladies and gentlemen unless to deliver a message or to ask a necessary question and then, do it in as few words as possible.
- Except in reply to a salutation offered, never say 'good morning' or 'good night' to your employer. Or offer any opinion to your employer.
- Whenever possible, items that have been dropped, such as spectacles or handkerchiefs, and other small items, should be returned to their owners on a salver [a dish].
- Never talk to another servant, or person of your own rank, or to a child, in the presence of your mistress unless from necessity. Then do it as shortly as possible and in a low voice.
- Never call from one room to another.
- Always respond when you have received an order and always use the proper address: 'Sir', 'Ma'am' 'Miss' or 'Mrs' as the case may be.
- Always keep outer doors fastened. Only the Butler may answer the bell. When he is indispensably engaged, the assistant, by his authority, takes his place.
- Every servant must be punctual at meal times.
- No servant is to take any knives or forks or other article, nor on any account to remove any provisions, nor ale or beer, out of the Hall.
- No gambling, or Oaths, or abusive language are allowed.
- The female staff are forbidden from smoking.
- No servant is to receive any Visitor, Friend or Relative into

the house, nor shall you introduce any person into the Servant's Hall without the consent of the Butler or Housekeeper.

- Followers are strictly forbidden. Any maid found fraternising with a member of the opposite sex will be dismissed without a hearing.
- No tradesmen or any other business having business in the house are to be admitted except between the hours of 9am and 3pm. In all cases the Butler or Chef must be satisfied that the persons he admits have business there.
- The Hall door is to be finally closed at Half-past Ten o'clock every night after which time the lights are out and the doors secured.
- The servants' hall is to be cleared and closed at Half-past Ten o'clock, except when visitors and their servants are staying in the house.
- No credit upon any consideration to be given to any person residing in the house or otherwise for Stamps, Postal Orders, etc.
- Expect that any breakages or damage in the house will be deducted from wages.

Not much of a life, is it? No swearing, smoking – or a hint of sex. In fact, the toffs are firmly convinced that the best way to keep the servants in line is to keep them working all the time – because the general belief is that if they are given time to themselves, they will indulge in the three Great No-Nos:

- Sex
- Alcohol
- Gambling

The fact that the male aristos indulge in these pleasures of life whenever they feel like it – and sometimes the sex is with the female servants – is irrelevant. What matters is the façade –

a well-run house with loyal, obedient servants – who only have sex if they're married. And, as we already know, marriage means 'goodbye job' for a female servant. When married, she will have her husband and children to look after.

RULES FOR THE SERVANTS WHEN ADDRESSING THE FAMILY

When – and only when – servants are permitted to address the family they have to always remember the following rules:

- The Master and Mistress of the house should be addressed as 'Sir' and 'My Lady'.
- The Eldest son of the family is addressed as 'Mister' (then his Christian name) and the youngest son as 'Master' (then his Christian name).
- When referring to the family in correspondence or speaking to a third party, always use the following form of address:

  'Sir John' (As in Sir John Pelham, for example)

  Lady Pelham

  Mister Pelham

  Master Pelham

  Miss Pelham.

- Greet all guests by their title and family name (as above) or as 'sir' or 'madam'.

THE EMPLOYMENT RULES: READING THE FINE PRINT

TIME OFF

By the late 1880s, servants start to get a bit more free time. Until then, they usually have to ask permission for any time off.

By the early twentieth century, servants are usually getting a half day off (on Sundays) and one day off a month, provided their chores are completed. They also get one week's holiday a year, which means that many try very hard to save up through the year to afford the train fare home for this one week – which is expensive on a servant's pay, if their own family are some distance away.

However, even during their time off, there are rules governing their behaviour both in the city and the country: they must return to the house by a set hour, usually around 9–10pm.

NO FOLLOWERS

A 'follower' is a boyfriend or young man, perhaps another servant from another family, who may be trying to court or woo a female servant.

Their presence is banned from the house to avoid even a chance of boy-girl pairing off – but human nature being what it is, such relationships still manage to flourish sometimes, usually when the family are away or not at home. Although below-stairs gossip, one of the few sources of free entertainment available and therefore incessant and sometimes bitchy, can still make breaking the 'no followers' rule a risky one to breach, even if a housemaid meets a boyfriend secretly in her time off.

There are, of course, exceptions to the rule: a few employers will actively approve a servant's marriage. But the idea of people in service forming close relationships is, for most employers, beyond the pale, especially if the servants both work in the same household.

PREGNANCY

No matter what the circumstances, a sacked servant carrying an illegitimate unborn child has nowhere to run. In 1911, nearly 50 per cent of illegitimate children are born to women working in service. City-based charities like the Girls Friendly Society do help illegitimate mothers, though many servant girls in this situation find there is no other refuge than to have their child in the workhouse, a grim option but often the only one.

The risk of unmarried pregnancy is high. There is no sex education. There is no contraception at all (the better-off in society are starting to find more effective ways to prevent pregnancy, but it's out of reach for the uneducated and poor). In a world where an unwanted pregnancy is always seen as the girl's fault, men don't carry any blame at all. And, of course, country-house employers don't want to lose their manual labour. It might mean an unpolished banister or a less-than-well-run kitchen. So, should they surface, the twin evils of sex and its consequence, unmarried pregnancy, must be banished from sight. Immediately.

THEFT

One of the big concerns of the country house employer is that any outsiders coming to the back entrance might be tempted to steal food. Or, a young servant might start sneaking food out of the house to an eager, but hungry follower. Hence the rules that apply to visitors or friends as well as to boyfriends. Given the amount of good-quality provisions around and the size of the household – and the quantity of food consumed – this is a very obvious temptation.

If anything at all goes missing in the house, all the servants' rooms or quarters are thoroughly searched, often by the butler. And if the missing item or items are found in a servant's possession, they are straight out of a job – without that all-important piece of paper, the reference, or 'character' as it's called.

THE CHARACTER

This is what we'd call a written reference. And all servants need a character to move from job to job. Without a character, no employment of any description is likely to be offered.

Not surprisingly, given the nature of much of the work, turnover of lower servants is quite high, though many middle-ranking domestic staff switch jobs, too. Upper servants do not move around as much. And it's not unknown for some families to keep their more valuable – even cherished – upper servants for twenty to thirty years. But if servants do want to move on, it's often for the usual reasons – more money, promotion, to expand their horizons or, as already seen, to find a suitable marriage partner. Yet if a servant is ambitious, he or she must be careful about moving around too much – two years or more is deemed a sufficient amount of time in one job – otherwise they can get a reputation for being 'short charactered', in other words, the characters he or she produces are revealingly brief, simply 'OK, did the job'.

The rule is: a servant must ask their employer, via the housekeeper or butler, for this 'character' to be written when they leave a household. And they do not get to see the contents; the document is forwarded straight on to their new prospective employer.

And if a servant is out of work for some time, perhaps because of illness or a family problem requiring their presence, it's very difficult to get back in once they step outside the country-house service network with no character to confirm they've been steadily working.

It's not unknown for a servant who hasn't worked for some time to send a begging letter to a house they've once worked in. The response, of course, would hinge on their relationship with their former employer. A woman who has left to marry and then finds herself widowed – not uncommon, given the lower life expectancy – will usually get a warm reception and be invited back into service. But only widows get this cordial treatment.

FINDING A JOB

By this time, there are two routes to employment in service that we are all familiar with: the printed advertisement in newspapers or magazines or the employment agency – more popular in the big cities where the middle classes have a greater turnover of domestic staff.

Yet for the country-house service roles, the toffs also have their own little hiring network if they need a new or replacement servant: the mistress of the house will write to her friends from other aristocratic families to let it be known that there's a vacancy coming up. Or she might write asking for extra information on a job-hunting servant currently working for another family – their own version of Linkedin (networking website for those employed in business), if you like.

There are a couple of other routes into a job in service. These are:

Being in a service family

Children of those already in service, usually in rural areas, are often seen as having good potential. These youngsters may have already started work at an early age, pre- teen years, maybe looking after an ageing local vicar or acting as an unpaid childminder. And country-house owners prefer rural servants to those from the bigger cities; they tend to be more hard working, more adaptable and less trouble.

The mobile servant network

A lady's maid or a footman tends to get around quite a bit in the course of their work, going to London, for instance during 'The Season', which means they get to meet other servants like themselves – and can keep in touch with each other, by letter, to find out when jobs at other country houses come up.

THE DINING RULES

The servants in the house have their food and lodging provided by their employer. But the rules around where and how they dine are equally as rigid as everything else.

The eating of main meals is segregated, according to the sex and status of the servant. Not only do the uppers and lowers never socialise together, they have separate rules for how they eat.

Senior servants – 'the Pugs' – traditionally eat in a separate Stewards' or Butler's room, waited on by lower servants, usually one or two footmen, with better food and drink than the lowers. They drink white wine, claret and beer at lunch and dinner. (Even the china, glass and cutlery they use may be of the finest quality, with napkins rolled into silver napkin rings at breakfast and lunch. At dinner, the napkins and table linens are changed.)

Yet by the early 1900s, in country houses like Downton Abbey, all the servants eat breakfast, dinner and supper in the servants' hall, a large area which is used both for eating and the lower servants' brief periods of leisure. (Outdoor staff like stablemen and gardeners tend to eat their meals as a group in their own communal dining areas.)

Table seating is according to rank. The butler sits at one end of the table, the housekeeper at the other end. The first footman sits to the right of the butler, the lady's maid sits to the butler's left.

Male servants sit in order of hierarchy down one side of the table, women according to their own status, down the other side. (At Anglesey Abbey in Cambridge, the servants' hall chairs are painted in a variety of colours, just to make sure they know where to sit.)

No one can sit down until the butler says so. When dining together in this way, everyone must remain silent – unless they are addressed by a superior.

THE SERVANTS' DINNER RITUAL

Dinner or supper (a later meal, after dinner, sometimes taken by the uppers or the family upstairs) is the most formal meal.

- A second footman rings a bell to announce dinner.
- The upper servants then congregate in the housekeeper's room. Then they walk, single file, down the corridor into the servants' hall in order of rank. The butler always leads the way (the first part of the Pug's Parade).
- At dinner, the butler carves the meat and sends the plate down to the housekeeper who then serves the vegetables. The footman takes the plates around – serving, of course, according to servant rank.
- After the meal, the upper servants march out, single file, to take their pudding, tea and coffee in the housekeeper's sitting room (the concluding part of the Pug's Parade). The first footman is then left in charge of the servants' hall.
- At certain grand houses, like Welbeck Abbey in Nottinghamshire, the uppers even dress for dinner like their employers. So any visiting ladies' maids or valets are required to do this too: the lady's maid in a 'dress blouse' (an evening blouse with lace inserts and elaborate pin-tucking) and the valet in a velvet smoking jacket.

THE FAMILY'S MEALTIME RITUALS

All meals are served at fixed times with set rituals for the family. Here's the timetable:

8am. The lady's maid and the valet wake their respective bosses carrying a special breakfast tray with tea and toast (or an arrowroot biscuit), a newspaper and any correspondence.

9.30am. Breakfast is served to the family in the dining room. Food is laid out in silver dishes, arranged across a long sideboard. All adult family members living in the house are expected to attend. The master sits at the head of the table, the mistress at the other end. The mistress pours the tea for everyone and the butler, after enquiring how everyone wants their tea served, hands the cups out.

9.15am. Everyone in the house is summoned by bell to the main hall for prayers, read by the master of the house, who may also make an announcement to the staff regarding a punishment – or a word of thanks. The session ends with the words: 'God make my servants dutiful.'

1pm. Luncheon The ladies enter the dining room first, two by two, followed by the gentlemen. Everyone is obliged to wear outdoor clothing or morning wear (for the women this means a tailor-made two-piece costume; for the men a morning dress coat, waistcoat, shirt, collar, tie and formal striped trousers).

5pm. Afternoon Tea is served in the Tea Room or the Drawing Room.

7pm. The sound of a dressing gong warns the family and their guests that it is time to go to their room to dress for dinner – in full evening wear. Dinner is the most formal and longest meal of the day.

8pm. Dinner The butler announces that dinner is being served. Family and guests make their way to the dining room.

Each gentleman offers his arm to a lady and they make their way to dinner in pairs. The master of the household leads the procession with the lady of the leading guest on his right arm, followed by the mistress of the house on the arm of the leading male guest. After dinner, the ladies retire to the drawing room and the men remain at the table, drinking and smoking. Depending on how many guests there are, dinner may last until 11pm or later.

RULES FOR TABLE MANNERS

At the dining table, guests and hosts alike must follow the correct etiquette for their manners at the table. Here are the most important Rules of the Table:

- NEVER take your seat until the lady of the house is seated.
- NEVER lounge on the table with your elbows, or tip back in your chair.
- NEVER play with your knives, forks or glasses. Cultivate repose at the table. It is an aid to digestion.
- NEVER tuck your napkin into your vest, yoke or collar. It is unfolded once and laid across the knees without a flourish. After the meal, at a restaurant or formal dinner, lay the napkin unfolded at your place. If you are a guest in the household and will remain for another meal, you may fold the napkin into its original creases.
- NEVER put the end of a spoon into your mouth; sip everything from the side of the spoon. Do this noiselessly.
- NEVER put your knife in your mouth, nor use a spoon when a fork will serve. Forks are used for eating ice cream and salad is folded or cut with the side of a fork, never with the knife. Even small vegetables like peas are eaten with a fork.
- NEVER hold your knife and fork in the air when your host is serving you afresh. Lay them on one

side of the plate when you send it to the host by
the servant.

- NEVER leave your spoon in a coffee or teacup. Lay it
on the saucer.
- NEVER cool food by blowing on it. Wait until it
becomes cool enough to eat.
- NEVER take a second helping at a large, formal dinner.
You will find yourself eating alone.
- NEVER make noise with the eating implements
against the china. Food must be eaten daintily, each
thing by itself.

THE COUNTRY HOUSE OWNER'S RULES

Life for the toffs is a series of obligations, rules and social
considerations. Here are five of the most important ones:

- The hosting of social events is, by custom, a priority for
the aristocratic elite and their circle. Their lives revolve
around wealth, privilege and politics. So drawing up guest
lists for these events is a crucial part of the social
networking which dominates their lives.
- The Shooting Party is a very important part of their social
lives. It can last for several days. Usually, it starts with the
master of the house hosting the shoot – but other activities
like fishing or hunting may be involved for guests.
- The children of the family are the only members of the
household who can move freely around the entire house,
above and below stairs. If the mistress wishes to inspect the
kitchen she arranges this via the butler.
- By custom, the children of the family live independently of
their parents. They eat only one meal – luncheon – with
their parents; other meals are taken in the schoolroom,
sometimes with a tutor or nanny. (Very small children

remain in the nursery, other than set times when they are brought down by staff to see the mistress.)

- Reputation is everything. Which means a reputation for moral fortitude is essential for the family. The master and mistress must ensure that chaperones are always present when all adult unmarried members of the family meet with the opposite sex. Failure to adhere to this reflects badly on anyone ignoring this rule, as well as on the household.

THE HOUSEHOLD CLEANING RULES

Even cleaning does not escape the rules. Certain jobs are only allocated to women, others to men only: it all depends on the value or status of what is being cleaned. Dusting and polishing expensive house furniture in the public rooms, for instance, is a male-only task carried out by footmen. These servants, hired for their visual appeal, also carry coals up and down stairs to dining rooms, drawing rooms, libraries and the most spacious bedrooms. Yet the other staircases, corridors and bedrooms in the house – those less visible to the eye – are cleaned by housemaids, who have to get down and dirty on the floor, scrubbing and grate cleaning.

Expensive glass, china, silver and mirrors are cleaned by footmen, while scullery maids wash all the utensils and cooking pots in the kitchen.

So pernickety are the Edwardian toffs, however, that even the dirtiest, muckiest jobs in the house are associated with things they'd prefer to ignore, like sex and bodily functions. So the laundry maid, whose work involves washing things like soiled bedlinen or the lengths of white muslin that act as sanitary towels (disposable ones remain way ahead in the future), and the lowest-ranking housemaid, whose work involves cleaning out toilets or chamber pots, are seen as being 'tainted' by their work – yet another reason why the aristos are so keen to keep such people 'invisible' at all times by restricting them to their own quarters and stairways. Talk about control freaks. If only they'd known about robots…

The laundry maid has other woes, too. Traditionally, laundries are sited in the least accessible, most isolated areas of the country house, because the work itself is so labour intensive and messy. Yet because these laundries are far away from prying eyes, laundry maids are a fraction more accessible and likely to be more 'at risk' from male attention than the other young women. And, of course, not all big country houses have yet switched to outsourcing their laundry in the early 1900s. So a 'follower' might, just, be able to creep in on the laundry maid unobserved.

Could you blame her if she actually welcomes the diversion?

BREAKING THE RULES

In a pre-Welfare State era, unemployment is equivalent to near destitution for the poorest people in society. So breaking the rules and being sacked, without any kind of reference, is disastrous: a life of crime, the workhouse, or for many young women, prostitution, are the only options.

When you consider that many young servant girls, especially in rural areas, are quite innocent in the ways of the world, this is tragically unfair: one very good reason why the rising tide of political pressure and campaigning for better rights for workers and women is beginning, albeit slowly, to make an impact in the early 1900s.

But right now, being thrown out of a poorly paid, back-breaking job and a life of rules and restrictions is disastrous: you are either locked into service – or out on your ear and destitute. It's a shamefully bad deal.

Servants sit down for dinner together in the evening.

KEEPING THEIR DISTANCE

One perfect example of the way the toffs maintain their distance from the servants is the method they use to receive messages or correspondence. When a letter arrives or a visitor leaves a calling card, only the butler or a footman can take it to the person concerned. But he cannot, at any time, merely hand it to them (even though he is wearing gloves).

Whatever the object, it must be first placed on a small silver tray (only ever used for this purpose) and the tray is then carefully handed to the recipient. Once the person has read it, they can, if they wish, place a reply on the same tray — and hand it back to the servant.

CHECKING FOR HONESTY

One way either the housekeeper or the lady of the house sometimes keeps a check on the standards of work of the housemaids is to hide a series of small coins in the rooms.

If a maid takes the money and keeps it, they are promptly sacked. If, however, the coins are not mentioned at all, it means they weren't cleaning properly so they are severely ticked off.

Chapter 5

Who Runs this House Anyway?

It runs like clockwork from just before dawn to the wee small hours. The grand country house is a veritable hive of incessant activity on a scale similar to that seen in today's finest luxury hotels; staff are cleaning, dusting, polishing, chopping, cooking, arranging flowers, gardening, stabling, greeting guests – the only difference between then and now is that the most pampered luxury hotel guests probably don't expect quite the same level of personal service, someone to help them dress, undress or shave, as you would find in the big Edwardian country house.

The rules and etiquette of behaviour are rigid. Yet not all country houses are run on exactly the same lines. Nor do they have the same number of servants. Or the same number of rooms. Some owners have already installed indoor plumbing and electricity – yet still don't permit the lower servants to use the flush toilets at night or have a bath more than once a week. Other families are more considerate of their staff's bodily needs. And some stubbornly insist on hanging on to the older, more labour-intensive ways of running the place rather than embracing the latest mod cons.

But with the family's status and appearance so high on the priority list, one thing matters above all: any visitor here must be suitably impressed with the smooth, orderly way the house runs.

Essentially, this is a showplace, a demonstration of the family's wealth and privilege. And that smooth running operation can only be achieved by the hard work of all the servant labour. Without the precisely calculated, hour-by-hour routine of the house, the whole thing becomes a shambles. And that must never happen…

Here is a brief rundown of a domestic schedule of the grand country house. It can, of course, vary – the family will, at set times of the year, be absent, visiting friends and family and socialising in London. And the pace of activity revs up when there are guests to be entertained with multi-course meals and shooting parties. But from the servants' perspective, an average day's work would run something like this…

THE HOUSE

The big grandfather clock in the hallway near the servants' quarters chimes 6am.

A 14-year-old housemaid in an attic room with sloping ceilings, shared with three other young housemaids who are reluctantly waking up too, gets out of a single, narrow iron bed and steps onto the bare wooden floorboards. A small table by her bed holds the candle that lit her way up a hundred stairs to an exhausted sleep the night before. On a washstand nearby sits a china basin and a big jug. Underneath her bed is a chamber pot, which will later be collected by an odd-job man or a very young hall boy whose role it is to empty the pots, take them downstairs and tip their contents into a covered slops bucket in the outdoor area.

Padding outside in her long nightgown, down the long, chilly corridor, she reaches a servants' bathroom. She and the other girls line up to fill their jugs with cold water, then hurry back to their room for a speedy wash, hands, face, underarms, private parts, before struggling into their underwear – knickers, pantaloons, corset – then the housemaid's workwear, a printed dress. Downstairs in the kitchen, the scullery maid has already been up since 5am, cleaning the grates in the vast kitchen, laying out the fire to heat the kitchen range, dusting and sweeping the kitchen in readiness for Cook's arrival, making sure everything from the night before has been cleaned.

By 6.30am the housemaids have climbed the several flights of stairs down to the backstairs basement kitchen area, running the entire length of the house, to start their first task of the day, preparing tea and toast for the housekeeper and the lady's maid.

Once they've delivered this, the housemaid's cleaning duties begin in earnest. They are busy opening the big shutters in all the ground floor areas, dusting and polishing the furniture, tidying up from the night before, sweeping the carpets in the big dining room, morning room and drawing room. (The general idea is that many of the rooms are cleaned and tidied while the family is still sleeping so that they don't run into the servants.)

At the same time, another housemaid is getting the fires going around the house, the coal from the coal room delivered by a footman, the wood or logs chopped the day before by the odd-job man.

7am. Cook is in her domain and the kitchen staff, including the scullery maid, are busily getting ready for breakfast, a main meal, which involves a lot of work. One kitchen maid is designated the task of getting the servants' breakfast ready.

Supervised by Cook, all manner of dishes are being prepared for the family: eggs, sausages, kippers, kedgeree, kidneys, bread, rolls – anything and everything the family might wish to eat. It's a busy time in the kitchen. And this is only the beginning...

8.15am. The servants get their hurried breakfast in the servants' hall: porridge, tea and bread and butter. The lady's maid, who has already taken her mistress's tea to her in her bedroom, must rush back upstairs again to run the bath, help her mistress dress and arrange her upswept hair. The butler, too, has already woken his master and will now be helping him shave, dress and prepare for the day. The brief breakfast over, the footmen start to lay the table out for the family breakfast. Upstairs, in the nursery, small children are already taking their breakfast with the nursery staff. A nursery maid has been up since 6am, cleaning and polishing the brass fireguard rails and bars before making the fires in the rooms. No one who works in this house gets a lie-in. Ever.

9.15am. Family prayers. The downstairs staff gather, either in the main hall of the house or, in some cases, where the house has its own chapel, they file into this room, for prayers to be read, first by the master of the house, then a prayer might be read by the butler. This is the only time the lowers get a glimpse of their masters, though they must adhere to the rules and not attempt to stare, make eye contact or initiate any communication with them.

9.30am. The family enter the dining room for their breakfast, the silver chafing dishes with their lids on already laid out on the huge sideboard. Breakfast is always overseen by the butler and footmen – though this is a meal where custom permits the family to serve themselves if they wish. The lowers carry on with their work in the kitchen and around the house while the family chomp their way through the big breakfast.

10–11am. Cook has embarked on organising the family's

lunch, issuing instructions to the kitchen staff, overseeing a huge roast on the cooking range, baking bread.

This is an important time of day for her: Cook and Housekeeper must, in turn, have their daily meeting upstairs with the mistress of the house; first the housekeeper goes into her parlour to tidy up and ventures upstairs. When she's finished, the mistress will see Cook to discuss menus. There's a lot for Cook to discuss – today's menu to be 'passed' by the mistress and what about tomorrow, how many dinner guests and what sort of meals will be required? (Menus are sometimes written in French, so staff have to know or learn the names of dishes in this language, as well as how to cook them perfectly.) And does Cook already have fresh produce from the estate and the kitchen garden? The housekeeper too has her daily directives; she must go through the accounts with her mistress. And there are questions she might have to answer: are the staff working properly? Is the new housemaid settling in?

Around the same time, the butler has his second meeting with the master of the house to discuss various arrangements: a meeting with the Estate Manager is scheduled today, the chauffeur is needed to take family members on a visit and there's a sensitive matter on the butler's agenda. The butler thinks a footman might be stealing food from the household. But he's not sure. He must be subtle; he can't exactly come out and approach his boss directly. But in judging his uncommunicative master's mood, he gleans that now is not the time to bring it up. He must wait and see what happens.

In the meantime, the lady's maid, having completed her mistress's toilette, is now in her own room, washing some silk underwear for her mistress. Then she must start trimming a big hat with feathers: the mistress wants to wear it to a local fête tomorrow.

Above, the cleaning activity continues. Now the first-floor

bedrooms are being cleaned by the housemaids: as soon as the family leave a room, the servants are free to go in to make sure that everything is as neat and tidy as possible. The housekeeper's standards are high but they need to be fast. Fortunately, today there are no guests staying overnight; this can make getting all the bedrooms clean in time tricky. Guests who stay mean extra work and if there are any late risers, getting all the work done is difficult – though everyone upstairs, guests or family, is expected to present themselves at the breakfast table.

It's an endless routine for which you need an army of working ants to get through: laundry to be collected and dispatched (to either the internal laundry area or an outside firm), carpets swept, with brush or sweeper, a daily battle with dust, paintwork washed, beds carefully made, mattresses turned; the bathrooms and toilets must also be rendered spotless.

Some items in the bedrooms must not be touched at any time. The dressing table in the mistress's bedroom is sacrosanct; it can only be cleaned and tidied by her lady's maid. And in the reception rooms below, expensive mahogany writing desks are only to be dusted by the butler.

This cleaning and tidying operation goes on every day. But given the size of the house, major super-cleaning sessions can only really take place when the family are away, during 'The Season'. Then the staff can clean thoroughly: windows can be left wide open for airing, the curtains, wallpaper and paintwork super-cleaned, all furniture polished to gleaming point – and there's enough of it to make this job a major exercise, hundreds of valuable items in expensive woods and fabrics, each armrest or leg to be rendered dust-free and spotless. Wall hangings, paintings, enormous mirrors have to be taken down and carefully cleaned, all drawers and cupboards tidied and lined with scented paper.

Downstairs in the butler's pantry, meanwhile, the first footman is busy polishing silver, the housekeeper has passed her food orders through to the suppliers and a local shopkeeper has already been and gone, delivering the previous day's orders at the tradesmen's entrance. Two housemaids are now taking the food deliveries for storage in the kitchen's huge larders. The head gardener has already organised supplies of fresh vegetables from the house's kitchen garden; an under gardener has also arrived with huge arrangements of fresh blooms from the garden – these will be placed in the hall and the public rooms by a footman or the butler. (If the mistress of the house is so inclined, she might indulge in some flower arrangement herself.)

Back in the kitchen, things are really starting to heat up. The scullery maid is frantically washing up all the breakfast pots and pans as Cook juggles the not inconsiderable task of supervising her staff to prepare lunch while she plans tonight's dinner and makes the next day's soup. In between her other duties, cooking vegetables, making savouries, sieving, chopping, pounding, a kitchen maid is also cooking the servants' main meal of the day, served at noon (and sometimes, confusingly, called dinner).

11am. Briefly, the servants have morning tea in the servants' hall. It's hardly a break because the housekeeper and butler, their meetings with their bosses over, are issuing yet more orders to the lower servants, before they scamper off to complete their various tasks. By now, the footmen are embarked on the table-laying process for the family's lunch. The kitchen staff are a whirl of activity: peeling, chopping, organising pans of boiling water; the scullery maid, too, is peeling a mountain of potatoes in the brief lull before the next lot of washing-up arrives.

12–2pm. The servants have their main meal in the servants' hall, then the butler, kitchen staff and footmen must be ready to serve the family lunch at 1pm sharp.

Today there are no guests, so lunch – a minor meal in the toffs' daily calendar – takes about an hour. The minute their bosses have finished and left the dining room, the entire to-ing and fro-ing process starts again in reverse: the table is cleared, the dishes and cutlery are taken, on trays, back downstairs. Today, the family's washing-up is being done in the butler's pantry, while the scullery maid must wash the servants' pots, pans and crockery, putting everything back in its right place – until the next meal.

For the fourth time today, the lady's maid is summoned away from her sewing to her mistress's side upstairs because she needs to change; she is going riding this afternoon. Out in the stables, a groom saddles the horse in readiness.

3pm–4pm. Cook and her team are preparing scones and cakes for the family's tea; Cook has also been bottling fruit and making jam from fruit collected from the estate. This is the one time of day when activity slows down somewhat for the lower servants. In theory they should get an hour to themselves in the servants' hall. Mostly they will chat, exchange gossip and sew, repair items of clothing or embroider. There might be time to write a letter home if they choose to go up to their rooms. But today, they stay put. They know there's every chance the upstairs bell will ring and there's something to be done for the family before tea is served to them at 4pm in the drawing room. Taken up by the footmen, the pretty plates, teacups, saucers and decorated cake stands are all neatly placed on small tables dotted around the room, where the tea-takers will perch on spindly chairs, as is the fashion. Then, once tea is finished, the footmen are back to clear everything away, an irritating task because there are so many small plates and dishes containing the cream, jam and butter precariously balanced on the tiny tables.

5–6pm. The kitchen basement area is a whirl of activity yet again: the servants get their evening meal at 6pm and dinner upstairs is scheduled for 8pm. The kitchen maid readies the servants' meal while Cook and her team run around busily getting the family's dinner ready.

The upstairs meal consists of up to six courses if the family is not entertaining, nearly double that number if there are guests in the house. Despite all the careful planning with the mistress, there are mishaps sometimes and sharp orders and raised voices from Cook if there are unexpected changes to the dinner arrangements. And the footmen need to know in advance how many places to lay out for dinner. Even one unexpected guest can be a problem because etiquette dictates there must be no unused settings at the table.

As the servants finish their final meal of the day in the servants' hall and the upper servants' quarters, Cook is supervising the presentation of a series of perfectly cooked and beautifully presented courses. Everything that goes on the dinner table must look beautiful as well as taste good. And the final presentation of the dishes is Cook's role and hers alone: the toffs and their elite group are very keen on garnish, so Cook must dress virtually everything they serve, even at breakfast, with a paper ruffle, a sprig of green, a time-consuming perfect glaze (a reduced stock that leaves an intensely flavoured, syrupy liquid used to decorate dishes) or another elaborate garnish.

7pm. The footman sounds the gong, the family must dress for dinner. The lady's maid attends her mistress upstairs – the fifth time today – helping her into her evening finery and redoing her hair – the riding session means it has to be redone accordingly.

8pm. The dinner is ready to be served. The footmen carry the huge trays of food upstairs into the dining room and the butler, after checking everything carefully before the dinner gong can be struck, oversees the ritual. The footmen carefully serve the wine (from the right) and the food (from the left). As the family dine, the housemaids are busy again, clearing up the bedrooms in the family's absence, picking up clothes, laying out nightwear, drawing the heavy brocade curtains, putting a stone hot-water bottle in the bed in winter. If there are guests staying in the house, both male and female staff must carry out this routine for each guest, another time-consuming task when the guest list runs into double figures – which it often does.

9–10pm. The scullery maid, exhausted, up to her neck in dirty crockery and suds, starts to tackle the final big washing-up session of the day. The kitchen maid is tackling the copper cooking pans and moulds (the moulds are frequently used for the dessert jellies), which must be cleaned thoroughly with a mixture of sand, salt, flour and vinegar. The copper utensils must be spotless. The housekeeper has a nasty habit of inspecting the copper pans set out on the huge kitchen dresser – and if they're less than perfect, there will be hell to pay.

The footmen, once they've cleared the dining room, can embark on cleaning the glass and cutlery once all the scullery maid's washing up is finished (even at this late hour, males and females must work separately). The butler cleans all the silver. And it's still not over for the scullery maid. She has to clean the flues, black-lead the cooking range, and clean the hearthstone, kitchen scullery and larder for tomorrow.

By now, the lady's maid and the butler have retired to the housekeeper's room for their nightly gossip. The lady's maid listens to the others, says little, and concentrates on her sewing. They are still, officially, on duty until their bosses have left the drawing room to retire for the night. Then, the lady's maid will go upstairs again to help her mistress prepare for bed. The butler too will be summoned to his master to make sure he has everything he needs before sleeping.

10.30pm–midnight. Finally, the long day draws to a close. The servants' door is locked and bolted by the butler. Every weary soul can retire to their sleeping quarters. Yet it's never really over, this non-stop attendance to their boss's every whim. Should any member of the family need anything at all once they're in their bedrooms, they can still, if they wish, ring the bell for a servant to rush to their side…

THE SETTING

The activity in the house is only one part of the story; the gardens and the estate that surround it must be run on equally ordered lines, so that the setting is equally awe-inspiring to the guests. And the country-house garden, by long tradition, supplies both the flowers that are used throughout the house (decorating the rooms and the dining table) and most of the fruit and vegetables prepared by Cook and her team. The kitchen garden, therefore, is an economically important part of the regular supply of foodstuffs to the house, as is the game the family regularly consume (the quail, venison, pigeon and hare) shot on the estate – sometimes in very large numbers, if a shooting party is organised.

Traditionally, the grand country house has a large stabling area, particularly in the years before the motorcar when transport was a horse-drawn carriage. Back then, a very large estate employed a head coachman, a second coachman and up to ten grooms, and maybe a dozen helpers and stable-hands. But in a house where a car and chauffeur had already been introduced, there are less horses in the stables – but grooms and stable boys are still needed because the family continue to ride – and, in some cases, horses are bred here for racing.

There are dogs, too, noisily making their presence felt. In country houses pointers, setters, Labrador retrievers or spaniels are best suited to the world of shooting and hunting. And huge mastiffs might be guarding stabling areas.

For the servants, of course, dogs wandering around the house itself can mean extra work, clearing up their mess or replacing torn items, small details which the housekeeper and her team must be up to speed to spot. And the important outdoor activities like the big shooting parties involve all the indoor staff, too: preparing for these is a big part of the organisational pre-planning that goes on all the time.

The gardeners and outdoor servants, however, have a slightly different deal to the indoor servants. They are paid wages. But they do not sleep or eat in the house. Their accommodation tends to be on the estate, in cottages. As a general rule, the younger staff – the under gardeners – live together in shared accommodation, sometimes with a maid or housekeeper who cooks or cleans for them. The head gardeners, stablemen, farmers and estate manager have their own cottages on the employer's land, in which they can live with their families. Their deal is far less restrictive.

But while they may be free from the day-to-day hierarchical rule within the house, their hours remain long, from 6.30am until it gets dark. And the work is endless and physically demanding.

In some big houses, the gardeners are divided up into separate teams, headed up by a supervisor or foreman. As well as a head gardener and six under-gardeners there may be a kitchen garden team, a fruit-tending team, a specialist plant team, another for bedding plants and a team exclusively devoted to cultivating flowers for the house. The gardener in charge of this gang will be cutting and arranging blooms to decorate the house and dining-room table every day.

When dinner parties are being organised, the head gardener is informed, via an upper servant, which colour flowers are required. Then he, or a gardener-cum-expert in creating flower arrangements, will make up the big arrangements in the greenhouse, securing the flowers with small bundles of rosemary twigs with raffia, so they can be fitted vertically into a container.

Then the decorations are taken in, via the servants' entrance, so that the butler or footmen can place them wherever they are needed. Big colourful bunches of sweet peas are popular, an emblem of Edwardian times: Edward VII even has one named after him – in crimson. And huge displays of roses and lilac are a must-have for fashionable hostesses.

When really big entertainments are planned, flowers are used to decorate all of the rooms in the house. At such times the gardening team will be around at the crack of dawn to get it all ready.

Given the toffs' obsession with decoration and appearance, the flower arrangements at the dining table are incredibly important: they contribute to the overall success of their dinner parties. Aristocratic hostesses vie with each other to create the most outstanding displays, often including exotic fruits like pineapples or perfectly ripe peaches wired into the flower displays. There are even external specialist flower arrangers, (usually a genteel woman from a respectable but impoverished background, much like the governess) who may be hired to come to the house to create lavish flower displays when needed. Sometimes the colours of the flowers at the table are chosen to match the dress of the Lady of the house. Attention to detail is all.

THE SEASON

For the landowning aristocrats and the new money elite, 'The Season' is the time they spend in London, in their town residence, to socialise and engage in politics. (Members of both Houses of Parliament participate in the Season.) Exclusive events, often including royalty, are held at the town mansions of the super-rich. And The Season is also a big opportunity for the toffs to formally introduce their children of marriageable age to society. (Women are introduced by presentation to the monarch at Court.)

The Season starts at Easter and ends officially on the Glorious Twelfth of August, when the shooting season for red grouse starts. After World War I, when elite society starts to change, the long Season becomes less important. As an important event on the social calendar, its significance peaks in the early years of the 1900s. Yet even today, remnants of The Season are still with us with events like Royal Ascot and the Henley Regatta.

TOOLS OF THE TRADE

Mostly, the servants' work in and around the house is very labour intensive. The steam irons, dishwashers, fridge freezers and other household appliances we take for granted are not yet around in the Edwardian era. But there are some helpful developments…

ICE

Artificial refrigeration is developed in the Victorian era and it is used commercially (to transport meat from the Antipodes, for instance). Yet it is largely mistrusted domestically until around 1903–4. Even then, many big houses don't use refrigerators. They either continue to use ice from open water on their own estate, taken by the servants to the kitchen area to be stored in large ice chests in a separate room. Or storage might be in an ice-well in the grounds of the estate. The housekeeper also has the option of ordering top-quality imported blocks of ice, often from Norway, which can be transported, via rail, to the house.

Ice is an important aspect of the dinner-table display, used in enormous moulds for ice cream and different shapes – ice swans are very popular – but only the handful of country houses who have adopted all the latest mod cons are using their own early versions of fridges.

CLEANING APPLIANCES

By 1903, early types of not-very-effective vacuum cleaners are available; 'vacuum cleaner parties' are held in London, where wealthy women sit and watch while the new invention is used in front of them. Yet the more efficient, mass-produced 'bag on a stick' upright vacuum cleaners, produced by Hoover in the US, are not imported into the UK until 1912. They are very much a luxury item, costing around £2 to buy, or 3/6d (three shillings and sixpence) a day to hire – only after World War II do they become more affordable for ordinary people.

WASHING AND DRYING

Soap is used in huge quantities in the big country house. Until the middle of the nineteenth century, soap is actually taxed, making it an expensive proposition for most. But by the dawn of the twentieth century branded soaps (like Sunlight) and washing powders are widely available and the washing process becomes slightly less time consuming than in the past.

Hand-operated washing machines with two wringers attached have also been available for some time. But laundry maids hate them because they are so heavy to operate when they are full. In the bigger houses – where the owner has installed their own plant to generate electricity – electrically powered washing machines are in use.

But these are the exception. Most houses now use a hand-operated washing machine for part of the laundry process and continue to run their own laundry. Some opt to use the big commercial laundries, usually in London, where the linens and laundry can be transported to the house and back by rail.

By tradition, there are big drying cupboards in the in-house laundry. But freshly washed items are also dried outdoors whenever possible – bleaching in the sun is important. Some laundry might be spread out on the grass, some on bushes or hedges. Clothes lines, made of hemp or wire, are useful, but stealing clothes from grass or lines became, over time, a common form of theft, so the laundress must be vigilant when drying outdoors – she doesn't want to have to report any losses to the housekeeper, whose role includes making an inventory for all laundry items – and keeping a sharp eye on any discrepancies.

She may be virtually unseen but the laundress is important to the success of the household routine: she needs to be an expert in every aspect of laundry: the washing, ironing, bleaching, drying and folding are equally

important and given the toffs' obsession with perfection –
and gleaming, crisp, white linen – there's no let-up in the
quest for pile after pile of dry, neatly ironed and pressed
linens in the cupboards.

STAIN REMOVAL

Before washing, all stains are removed by the laundry
maid or lady's maid. Shop-bought cleaners are not used
on stains because they are acid based and quite dangerous
to the very delicate silks, cottons and linens that are used:
clothing made from man-made fibres emerges in 1910
but the aristocracy, whose clothes are often handmade and
who sleep in sheets of the very finest linen, are unlikely to
embrace such developments.

Here are a few useful stain removal methods used by
country house servants:

Wine stains: Wet the stain with cold water. Then
sprinkle it with dry starch and rub into a paste. Avoid
washing with soap beforehand as this will fix the stain.
Leave the paste to dry for an hour. The stain should then
be gone when the paste is rubbed off. If it's a stubborn
stain, salt and lemon juice rubbed on for a few minutes,
then removed by pouring hot water through it, will get
rid of it.

Blood stains: Wash in cold water if the garment is wet.
If it's dry, soak the garment in cold water with added
washing soda. Then wash it as usual and dry in the open.
Starch paste may also be useful in removing bloodstains.

Fruit stains: Pour boiling water over the stain. Avoid
using soap – it will fix the stain.

Ink stains: If the ink is still wet, sprinkle the item with salt. Then rub with a cut lemon. Another method is to soak the item in sour or boiled milk; as the stain is absorbed into the milk, renew the milk. Or try rubbing the stain with a tomato cut in half.

FROM THE COUNTRY HOUSE GARDEN...

Create your own scented Edwardian delights using these two easy ideas:

Rose water (a very popular Edwardian scent). Place some freshly gathered rose petals in an enamel pan, cover with water and very slowly bring the mixture to the boil. Simmer for ten minutes. Then strain the water into a jug or bottle. Use as a facial toner or on irritated skin, for an anti-ageing, rejuvenating effect. (You can also make chamomile water, which also helps firm skin tissue, by soaking chamomile flowers in water and shaking twice daily for two weeks. Then it is ready to be strained and bottled.)

Potpourri: essence of rose. Potpourri is a mixture of dried flowers and other ingredients which, when combined, create a delicate aroma. Flowers that are good for potpourri are roses, carnations, violets, sunflower and lavender. Good herbs include chamomile, sage, thyme, lavender and rosemary. Eucalyptus leaves are also very aromatic.

For Essence of Rose you need:
- 1 cup dried pink rose petals
- half a cup dried red rose petals
- half a cup dried white rose petals
- quarter cup chamomile flowers
- half a cup crushed statice (blue or white sea lavender)
- half a cup eucalyptus leaves

- quarter cup of oak moss
- 20 drops rose oil

Method:
- Combine petals and leaves in a large bowl.
- Using an eyedropper, scatter drops of rose oil over the mixture.
- Stir carefully. Then place the mixture in a brown paper bag lined with wax paper. After folding the bag, seal it with a paper clip.
- Leave it to dry in a dark, cool, dry place for two weeks.
- Stir the contents gently to blend it all every second day.
- Place the mixture in small dishes or glass bowls topped with tiny pink or white dried rose buds.

Scented paper (to line drawers and shelves). Using wrapping paper or unwanted sheets of wallpaper for the lining, place the sheets of paper in a large polythene bag – and sprinkle over the blended potpourri. Seal the bag, shake occasionally and leave until you're ready to line the drawers or cupboard shelves with the paper for a beautiful, subtle scent.

NATURAL REMEDIES

Repeated washing up in soapy suds mean that servants' hands can become chapped and sore. For this reason, they often cover them with black gloves when out and about.

Here's a simple remedy for chapped hands...
Rub honey into your hands when the skin is dry, moisten a little, rub harder, then use a little more water. Finally, wash hands thoroughly with the water still containing traces of honey, or wash hands with soap and rub them well with oatmeal while wet.

Swollen feet or ankles are another occupational hazard in service. This natural remedy is very useful...
Bathe or soak feet in a mixture of half water and half natural apple cider vinegar. Wrapping feet in a cloth that has been soaked in this mixture will also help ease the swelling.

Chapter 6

Relationships

Here we are in an idyllic setting, a vast house in the peace and tranquillity of the countryside. But is the perfection of the landscape matched by the warmth of the day-to-day relationships of the people living inside? Do they get on? Are they close? Are there strong bonds and friendships?

Hopefully, there are sometimes. By our twenty-first century standards, these relationships are difficult to fathom: servants with no real life of their own constantly running hither and thither at their master's whim; wealthy landowners whose lives are dominated by matters of inheritance – yet who see very little of their children; mothers who relinquish the baby-bonding process to hired help; relatives whose primary concern is rank, political manoeuvring, or marrying off their heirs into equally rich families.

We are in an odd world of marriage negotiations for fat dowries, entertainment on a grand scale mainly for social position, servants who are snobs because they earn their living by a strange mixture of deference and ordering other servants about. Are there any normal, everyday human relationships in such a world? Let's look more closely at some of these.

THE ARISTOCRATIC MARRIAGE

The fictional *Downton Abbey* marriage is one of many similar 'arrangements' of the times – it starts out as a 'cash for title' deal: rich and beautiful young American girl marries Earl who really needs her money to swell his dwindling resources.

Yet the relationship develops. Gradually they grow close – and loving. So much so that the Countess of Grantham conceives – and loses – a male heir after their three daughters have grown up. With this as an example, it seems that Edwardian aristocratic marriages might be similar to all marriages – some work, some don't.

But that isn't quite the case. Not all aristocratic marriages are cold, sterile, unhappy affairs: marrying for love isn't completely unknown. And, like the Granthams, some marriages begin as a trade-off for cash and status, yet they do work over time, though quite often, unlike the Granthams, they wind up as friends rather than lovers.

However, a lot of these 'arranged' marriages, or marriages of convenience, do not work at all when the main objective is money and inheritance rather than love and desire. Once the woman has fulfilled her part of the deal – by producing 'the heir and the spare' – there's often an end to any physical relationship. Separate bedrooms are common. Affluence and privilege mean that these couples don't need to retain any personal intimacy with each other if they prefer a 'hands-off' relationship after children are born. The focus of their world, remember, is not on romantic love – it's on the clearly defined rules and role-playing which dictate practically every minute of their lives. And, of course, inheritance.

Rich as she may be, the aristocratic wife cannot have an independent role outside the boundaries of the rules, other than as a kind of superior manager of the household. Apart from this, she can only involve herself in charitable concerns. She may be important but hers is a fairly restricted job description.

Essentially, she is close to what we'd call a Trophy Wife. She is required to be attractive, dress beautifully in the very latest styles and look fashionably alluring at all times – a living reflection of the wealth and influence of her husband. She can be intelligent – but she can't be too clever. In some ways, she is very much akin to her children in the nursery – seen at set times but not heard too much. Conversationally, on a social level, she is expected to make witty, light conversation. But nothing too deep.

If she doesn't have great interest in the day-to-day running of the household, she can, if she chooses, leave much of it to the housekeeper. And if she is politically minded, interested in women's rights and drawn to such worldly matters, she may, if she is bold enough, involve herself with such things – but only up to a point because she's probably going against her husband's wishes, so needs a strong will to do so. Her status as part of a power couple is more important than anything else.

The rules of the aristocratic marriage mean that the couple are rarely in each other's company anyway. They dine together at home and when they entertain. They accompany each other to all the big events of the Season, the parties, balls and concerts where they are obliged to be seen together – as well as the local events like the fund-raising fêtes. But that's it. When at home in the country, most of their time is spent apart – he in his study or on the estate, tending to his affairs, she paying courtesy calls to friends or relatives or visiting the poor (in between those lengthy sessions with her lady's maid as she changes her outfit and hairdo several times each day). And when the social clique moves to

London, through the summer, her husband will frequently spend a great deal of time at his club of choice, maybe the Carlton or White's or, if he's a working MP, at the Houses of Parliament. In so many ways, theirs is a marriage in name only.

So is there a get-out clause? Unfortunately, divorce is not really on the agenda. Despite their fabulous wealth and luxury surroundings, a divorced woman, middle class or aristocratic, faces a problem: her valuable social status vanishes if she's no longer officially part of a couple. Everyone, including her family, rejects her.

So how, you wonder, do such unhappy or loveless aristocratic marriages continue to survive?

There are a couple of reasons – aside from the very restricted status of all women at the time. In the world they live in, constantly surrounded by servants, a 'private' life for anyone seeking extra-marital dalliance is somewhat difficult to maintain. You need your peer group to turn a blind eye and maybe servants whom you hope you can trust (not a very reliable premise). And so when either he or she seeks some sort of romantic or sexual satisfaction in their lives, it's unofficially yet widely accepted among their chums that society will politely turn away from openly criticising any infidelities.

The other thing that holds the whole thing together, of course, is the very nature of their lifestyles. Because of the way they live, together but apart, provided they fulfil their many social obligations as a couple, the 'You live your life, I live mine' deal is something many can live with. Yet again, as with the rest of their lives, only appearance matters.

PARENTAL RELATIONSHIPS

Though there are exceptions, in many aristocratic households the parent-child relationship is emotionally distant and very much hands off: child rearing does not feature in the duties of an aristocratic woman – the servants, nurses, tutors, nannies and governesses fulfill most of that role. As tiny tots, a set time of day is set aside for the children to be brought down from the nursery to see their parents, usually around 4pm or after dinner and, once a son reaches eleven, sometimes sooner, he is packed off to boarding school while his sisters remain at home to be educated by a governess or tutor.

Yet if the aristocratic wife is a hands-off mum for much of the time, her partner, preoccupied as he is with his estate, his politics or his outdoor pursuits, is frequently even more remote from his children: the 'Distant Dad' is the kindest way to describe him, an unknown and often unseen authority figure. Some high-born mothers do develop a closer rapport with their children, over time. But essentially, the younger parenting years are left to the hired help.

But there is sometimes one loving and caring relationship in all this: the children's nanny. Though there are exceptions – nannies whose demeanour is cold, even ferocious – a good nanny is likely to form a close bond with the aristocratic children in their charge: a source of love and support that many children, semi-ignored in this bewildering world of appearance and convention, treasure and cherish, even cling to, as they grow up. And the children, of course, are the only people in the big country house who might sometimes climb downstairs, so they can have some sort of familial relationship with those below stairs.

Nanny is often valued. In some country houses with big families, she is kept on as an employee in the house, with different duties, even when the children have grown up. She is, effectively, a surrogate mum. And often a good one at that. Yet her status remains fixed: she may be loved, even adored by 'her' children, someone to cuddle and nurture them at all times, someone to guide them, to trust and confide in. But she's still a servant.

Even her earnings don't reflect her true value to the family: she usually earns less than the housekeeper. Or the chef. It's an odd world, for while good behaviour and manners are high on the list of the privileged person's rules, the emotional wellbeing of their children, as we understand it, isn't really a priority.

As siblings, of course, the children sometimes form close relationships with each other, particularly in the nursery years before the boys are packed off to boarding school. Some form lifetime bonds. Others are quite detached in their relationships with each other. The regimented nature of their existence and the huge distinction between the sexes, where only the boys really 'matter' in the aristocratic world, can create resentments as they grow older. Many younger aristocratic women are already rejecting the limitations of a world where only the 'right' marriage and having sons matters: at the turn of the century (in 1900) a third of all peers' daughters remain single.

So there it is, relationships, Toff style: husbands and wives leading separate lives, children nurtured by surrogates, only siblings sometimes forming closeness with each other. Is the master-servant relationship any different?

THE MASTER-SERVANT RELATIONSHIP

THE UPPERS

While some aristocratic wives have a good relationship with their housekeepers and rely on them heavily, it is the lady's maid who ventures the closest to what we'd call a close relationship with her boss, partly because of the nature of her work, and also because women, by instinct, have a greater tendency to confide in each other.

At times, a lady's maid might be her mistress's confidante. The lady of the house will correspond with friends and relatives of equal status and share her concerns or thoughts with them but on a daily basis, the lady's maid is the person with whom she chats and discusses her concerns about her children, her husband, her worries big and small.

Occasionally, a lady's maid will know more than anyone else in the house – even the master – about the woman she serves because if she's really trusted, she'll hear quite a lot about her boss's secrets – and what is going on generally within the family. In turn, her mistress will sometimes ask her maid for her views, though it's more likely to be her opinions on the latest fashion or the nicest hat to buy than anything else.

If the lady's marriage is a sexless arrangement and she is tempted towards or indulging in other liaisons or flirtations, the lady's maid may possibly be aware. (Just as if her boss is pregnant, she'll be the first to know, since she washes all her undergarments.) The lady's maid performs so many personal tasks, washing and arranging her boss's hair, running her bath, helping her dress, travelling with her, that she's privy to a great deal of information. She's more than a PA, but a shade less than a chum.

This puts her in a very odd position because the boundaries of deference are always there, day in, day out. If she repeats what she hears, she risks her job should she be found out. And yet there's a good chance that she won't. Sometimes it's quite easy for a gossipy lady's maid to repeat the things she's been told to someone downstairs, and for the gossip to then be passed on, by other staff, to people outside, like tradesmen. Then the gossip and the stories will go beyond the house, right across the county, a local version of email or Facebook, if you like. And because the toffs' world of rules is so regimented, quite often they're unaware that this is actually happening:

many don't even regard their servants as human beings, even though their etiquette always warns them: 'servants have eyes and ears to wag downstairs'.

More enlightened families, of course, don't see their servants as inhuman (again, the Granthams are sometimes good role models for how to treat your servants), but many view servants as little more than robots. And so a dinner-table conversation where butlers or footmen must stand, outwardly impassive, yet with ears flapping, taking in every word, all too often winds up as good fodder for downstairs gossip to spread beyond the estate. So a nosy servant who loves to gossip – and relishes the little bit of 'power' this gives them – may seem to risk much. But they know the chances are high their bosses will never know what is being said about them. The real downstairs currency isn't cash – it's gossip about other people living in the house.

Gossip aside, many loyal and trustworthy upper servants remain proud of their hard work and their relationship by association with their bosses, especially butlers or valets whose loyalty and feelings for their masters can often be strong, especially if they are valued.

Even after they leave the job, some upper servants will keep in touch by letter. But the uppers are the servants with staying power, sometimes working with a family for many years, giving them more opportunity to develop closer links with their employers. But even with this 'insider' access to their employer's lives, they must always, at all times, stay on their side of the line; even after years of service, they can't start a conversation or initiate a topic for discussion. They still have to wait to be asked.

THE LOWERS

Generally speaking, the lower servants, some footmen, kitchen staff and housemaids, don't form any relationship of any description with their masters. They don't have face-to-face dealings with them as such; many don't stay in their posts for any length of time, often opting to move around from job to job. Many young women take a position in a big household for opportunistic reasons – because they know it will teach them the household duties and skills they need for marriage. Then, once they find a marriage partner, they're gone. Many footmen don't see it as a job for life either, given the restrictions.

The lowers also move jobs a lot because that's the only option available to them if they dislike their employers or become angry and resentful of their behaviour. The only other way to 'get back' at their bosses – apart from passing on nasty gossip – is to steal from them. There's plenty of temptation, after all, with so much valuable stuff all over the house. Court records show lots of examples of lower city-based servants stealing – yet not that many steal from country houses. Servants might smuggle out a bit of food for their family, but this goes by largely unnoticed.

Yet the most difficult, and often poisonous, of all the relationships in the country house – and what affects servants even more than the attitudes of their bosses – is frequently the relationships they have with each other.

Bad behaviour from co-workers can have a powerful impact on some servants. Because people work so closely for such long hours with little time away from one another, they are forced to tolerate each others' shortcomings. Combine this with the snobbish distinction the uppers maintain over the lowers and you have a recipe for edginess, tension, unhappiness – and rows.

As in modern office politics, one viper in the nest can easily make life hell for the rest. And there's no HR or personnel department to fight their corner. If a housemaid wants to tell tales on a colleague's behaviour to the other servants after a petty row, there's nowhere to run. Breaking rank or running to the housekeeper with such tittle-tattle could mean being shown the door. Quickly.

Yet some of the younger housemaids sharing their attic bedrooms do bond with each other. They form friendships, simply because they need to: they're all living in each other's pockets all the time. Many of these youngest girls have an awful time emotionally, particularly if they're new to service. A combination of missing the familiar world of family while another servant makes their life hell with bullying behaviour or putting them down in front of the others all the time, is enough to make many homesick young girls desperate to run away. Some do just that, never to return. But a pleading letter home to family, asking to return home, will often receive short shrift: any money the girl can save from her meagre earnings is more important to her family's survival than her battle putting up with the worst of her colleagues' behaviour.

For the servants, emotional support (in the form of letters) from their family may often be all they have if their relationships with each other are poor. Yet even this correspondence can be difficult to maintain on a regular basis. For a lady's maid or butler, for instance, moving around with the boss means that family communication is sometimes broken or erratic. Changing jobs might not help either – a servant with a good 'character' might secure a better position, say a promotion from senior housemaid to housekeeper, yet wind up living even further away from their loved ones.

Some considerate employers help with small things, like the cost of postage. And some do allow close family members to 'visit' for a meal in the servants' quarters or even, occasionally, an overnight stay in the house. But usually, personal contact with family is a one-off annual event: a train ride to see them – and often to find their loved ones living in cramped conditions with little to eat.

RELATIONSHIPS BETWEEN UPPERS AND LOWERS

The innate snobbery of many of the upper servants – governesses, for some reason, can be particularly snobbish towards the lowers, perhaps because they are acutely conscious of their mid-ranking status, neither lower class or quite middle – means that relationships between uppers and lowers is, at best, functional. The rules are always there. Being forbidden to speak at mealtimes, for instance, unless an upper addresses you directly, doesn't do much to foster good relationships, especially if you're a young and vulnerable new recruit. The best you can say about these social situations is that the lowers are very much the apprentices, there to learn the ways of service. And if they're willing to work hard, they might be fortunate enough to have an upper servant supervising them who appreciates their diligence. Provided they keep quiet and don't break a single rule.

THE UPPERS' RELATIONSHIPS

Surely the uppers have some sort of relationship with each other? They do – yet they are more what you'd call work cronies than friends because of the nature of their jobs. The effective bosses of everything downstairs, the butler and housekeeper, do wind up sharing their daily experiences and views in the housekeeper's sitting room – probably because they can't express them openly to anyone else – unless the butler has a wife and family, of course, which isn't often the case.

Given the huge amount of work that has to be completed and delegated each day, they rely on each other, to an extent, to share their woes. They are their own little clique. Which is probably why the lowers resent them so much.

SEX AND SERVANTS

Despite all the restrictions around followers, a job in a big house is regarded by many young female servants as a way of meeting eligible young men, despite the very limited amount of time off. These young men are usually servants in other households or young shop workers or tradesmen who come to the house, their equals in society. And once a link or attraction is established, they can maintain contact by letter. Other lower servants like footmen aren't expecting to stay single either, so they tend to be on the lookout too. And not all employers are completely rigid in forbidding their servants to form relationships with the opposite sex: sometimes families do permit a female servant to invite her young man to tea in the servants' quarters. It's just not a commonplace scenario.

As for sex between servants in the house, while the toffs do everything in their power to ensure this does not happen, they can't overcome the power of sexual attraction – and human nature. It might mean a lot of subterfuge and secrecy, given the penalties of unemployment without references if they're caught. But at times a willing young girl will give rein to her impulses. And, of course, there are always the unwanted advances: the randy footman who pushes a girl into a corner and won't take no for an answer, and a master – or his sons – who use female servants for sex.

This is a stereotypical view of servants – yet it seems that Sex with the Servants is something the ruling classes often see as their prerogative: a famous erotic book, *My Secret Life*, published in 1888, is the detailed sexual memoir of an anonymous but very sexually active gentleman. The book makes it very clear that the writer regards female servants as sexual playthings, 'ready for service'.

Frequently, aristocratic parents are all too conscious of this sexual temptation with young housemaids around. And they make quite deliberate efforts to keep their younger sons away from attractive young women working in the house: a new hiring of a really pretty young servant, for instance, is often seen as A Very Bad Idea if there are young sons in the house – to the extent that it's not unknown for families to dispatch sons to boarding school as early as possible to avoid this kind of temptation. So much effort goes into keeping the sexes separate in the country house. But there are many times when all this effort is in vain.

GETTING MARRIED

Sometimes a liaison between servants will lead to pregnancy. Whether they marry or not – and some do – it's usually the end of their time in the house, though the male servants might be able to remain working in the household. Butlers, footmen or valets can take a wife, but then they have the problem of finding a home for themselves and their family. If their employer provides a home located on the estate, that's fine, though it may still create an accommodation problem if they wish to move to another employer. And, of course, if their family home is sited some distance away, it may mean living under their employer's roof still – yet seeing little of their wife and kids. If servants wish to marry in secret and keep quiet about it, they might stay under the same roof – but that doesn't happen very much.

Married housekeepers? Not really wanted, thanks. As stated before, if they're unexpectedly widowed, however, they're often welcomed back into the household. Even the lady's maid, well travelled and often better versed in the ways of the world than other servants, can't marry and keep her job. So there aren't too many examples of servants marrying each other. Given all the rules and the long hours worked, is it so surprising?

DIVORCE: THE PENALTY

In 1913 just 577 divorces are granted in England and Wales. Divorce is avoided at all costs because it means scandal. It is expensive. It completely destroys an aristocratic woman's reputation. And the divorce laws of the day are complex and very much in favour of the husband. A divorced woman carries a heavy social stigma: she is shunned by her elite circle – the invitations to the posh balls and lavish dinners dry up. In the phrase of the day, she is 'cut' by all the people she knows. She often suffers financial losses and she may even lose out where her children are concerned – access to them can be denied her. So while only the very wealthy can access divorce, few do.

ADULTERY MAKES YOU MAD

One bored aristocratic woman who pays a severe penalty for her extra-marital dalliance with several men in her circle, including Edward VII, then Prince of Wales (known as 'Bertie' or the less flattering 'Tum Tum' as he aged), is Lady Harriet Mordaunt, daughter of a Scottish baronet and the beautiful young wife of a prominent MP, Sir Charles Mordaunt. After Harriet confesses to sleeping with Bertie – and other men – her enraged husband threatens to name the Prince of Wales as a co-respondent in what then becomes the most scandalous divorce case of the late Victorian era. Their country house, the 72-bedroom Walton Hall in Warwickshire, is, at the time, the most talked about stately home in the land. The Prince finally appears in court as a witness – yet coolly denies sleeping with Harriet. And her family, in a desperate attempt to preserve their honour, declare Harriet insane.

After the divorce, Harriet is committed to a lunatic asylum, where she remains for the rest of her life. She dies in 1906. And Sir Charles re-marries – to 16-year-old Mary Cholmondeley, a parson's daughter.

TURNING A BLIND EYE

One semi-detached marriage where an aristocratic husband is extremely tolerant of his wife's behaviour is that of the Countess of Warwick, Frances Maynard, otherwise known as Daisy, and the Earl of Warwick, Francis Brooke (known as 'Brookie'). Daisy has a string of lovers and admirers after their marriage in 1881. Beautiful, indiscreet and notorious everywhere for her scandalous love life (she is one of Edward, Prince of Wales's favourite mistresses until she breaks off their relationship with the news that she's expecting another man's child), she inspires the music hall song 'Daisy, Daisy'.

Yet she remains married to 'Brookie' until his death in 1924 – after 43 years of marriage. At one point, friends are told he would rather have been married to Daisy 'with all her peccadilloes' than any other woman in the world.

Extravagant and reckless, Daisy's later years are overshadowed by money problems – at one point she tries – and fails – to sell her love letters from the King after his death. Yet despite her lurid love life, Daisy has a strong social conscience and becomes very involved with helping the underprivileged, unsuccessfully attempting to stand as a Labour MP in 1923. She dies, age 76, in 1938.

A SECRET MARRIAGE

A gentleman might wish to take advantage of a housemaid's physical charms. But in such a status-conscious society, very few would venture to marry a servant. Yet there are exceptions. Hannah Cullwick is a domestic servant from Shropshire whose working life in service began at the age of eight. While working in an aristocratic household in London, she meets Arthur Munby, a gentleman civil servant with an obsession for documenting the lives and behaviour of women in service – especially those whose work involved hard physical labour. They marry in secret, in 1873.

Hannah lives in her husband's home as his servant – and insists he continue to pay her wages. In diaries she calls herself her husband's 'drudge and slave' and for most of her life wears a leather strap around her wrist and a locking chain around her neck – to which only Arthur has the key. Hannah also has a fascination with cleaning boots, sometimes licking them clean. At one point she informs Arthur she could tell where her master has been – by how his boots taste. They split up and Hannah moves back to work in the country, but they continue to see each other until she dies in 1909. Their secret marriage, recorded in detail in their respective diaries and letters, is only revealed to Munby's brother just before Arthur dies in 1910.

FUN WITH THE SERVANTS

Viola Bankes grew up in Kingston Lacy, Dorset, the 8,500-acre country estate and family home of the aristocratic Bankes family, the owners of Corfe Castle, destroyed in the English Civil War in 1646.

Growing up in the huge, beautiful seventeenth-century estate – boasting eleven working farms and three villages – Viola and her siblings Daphne and Ralph see little of their good-looking parents, Henrietta and Walter Bankes, whose lives revolve around entertaining high society and the social round of the London Season. Walter dies in 1904. Yet his children are not told that their father has died. Only five years later, when a servant mistakenly blurts out the truth, do they hear what has happened: their father, knowing he is dying of heart disease, has told them he is going abroad to India. In fact, he hides at home, in his huge four-poster bed – two flights of white marble stairs below his wife's room.

With their widowed mother largely preoccupied with running the house and the estate, the three Bankes children rely on the Kingston Lacy servants for emotional support – the family butler, Mr Cooper, even gives them pocket money as part of his duties. Viola loves spending time with the servants, playing billiards and whist with them, sliding on the vast polished floors for fun. In her memoir, *A Kingston Lacy Childhood*, Viola writes: 'I climbed on Edith's strong broad back whenever she was on all fours dusting the oak boards, which cannot have helped her in her work.'

As the children grow up, their bonds with the live-in staff grow stronger. 'It was not our parents, but our governesses on whom our happiness most depended,' writes Viola.

KIND & CARING EMPLOYERS

One country house estate, Erddig Hall, in Wrexham, has a long history of very good master-servant relationships, treating its servants with kindness and respect. Many of its staff serve with the Yorke family for much of their working life: Jane Ebbrell, who works as a housemaid for the family her entire life until her nineties, is retained on the payroll when her domestic duties end as a 'spider brusher' (the person responsible for brushing the cobwebs). In a period spanning the eighteenth to twentieth centuries the Yorkes celebrate their servants' lives in poetry and even commission a series of portraits of their staff. These portraits still hang in the downstairs area of the house. They include portraits of a housemaid, coach boy, gamekeeper, gardener and a blacksmith. Remarkably, two tributes to former butlers are displayed on special hatchments (squares or lozenge-shaped panels or tablets, used to commemorate the death of the bearer). Traditionally, hatchments are only used to commemorate the gentry and their ancestry, a genuine mark of respect for their much-loved servants.

The Countess of Warwick in her car circa 1905.

Chapter 7

Food & Drink

WHAT THEY EAT UPSTAIRS...

Food. The very finest: truffles, oysters, caviar, game, langoustine, lobster, asparagus, guinea fowl, sirloin steak, soufflés, patisserie, pâtés, soups, desserts, course after course after course, cooked, boiled, grilled, cold, hot, served every way you can think of, covered in rich sauces, high glazes and pretty garnishes. You name it, the Edwardian elite eat it, often sourced from their own farmlands or shot on their estates – to be served on showily decorated, vast dining tables covered with crisp, snow-white linen, presented on costly silver dishes, eaten off the finest Wedgwood china, and washed down with the best wines, champagnes, ports and liqueurs served in sparkling crystal glasses.

It's all so elaborate: enormous multi-coloured jellies that shimmer and sparkle in the light, petite pastry boats filled with colourful seasonal berries, ice-cream moulds shaped like pairs of cooing doves, carefully garnished with maidenhair ferns.

Bonbons displayed on high stemmed dishes; creamy gateaux, enormous fruit baskets dotted along the tables. Pretty, decorative, alluring food displays. And that's just dinner.

In fact, large quantities of food are served in the country house throughout the day; low-fat calorie counters need not attend. Showoffs, however, reign supreme. What you eat, how you eat it and, most importantly, where and with whom you dine or invite to your dinner table, are all of the utmost significance: food as status symbol, yet another way of showing the world your elevated position.

In some big houses, hostesses are judged purely on the talent of their ultra-fashionable chef: French, overpaid and frequently temperamental in the kitchen. Who cares if he rubs the kitchen staff up the wrong way? It's his presence – and skills – that matter. Food is the ultimate social test; reputations can be ruined in the course of one evening if the meal or service isn't perfect. And in the Season, the fashionable must see and be seen dining in London's newest and smartest hotels, the Ritz, the Savoy, or the Prince of Wales's favourite restaurant, Rules, in Covent Garden, where he regularly occupies his own intimate velvet-swagged dining room to wine and dine his favourite mistresses like Lily Langtry; love and laughter accompanied by huge, blow-out, twelve-course meals, with lashings of French champagne and wine. And lots of cigar smoke. (Rules and the Café Royal rent out private dining rooms by the hour for toffs in search of a bit of privacy with their latest squeeze.)

Edward's gluttony, his love of everything French, particularly food inspired by the French culinary guru, artist and craftsman Escoffier (the Heston Blumenthal of his day but with a sexy French accent), sets the fashion for all upper-crust dining: it is excessive, highly structured and completely over-the-top, the last time in Britain's culinary history that society will participate in such foodie indulgence in this way.

Compare this calorie-laden extravaganza to the diet of the very poorest working families. Their daily menu usually consists of tea, bread and jam for breakfast and a dish of potatoes with bacon later in the day. Meat or fish is, at best, a weekly luxury. And that is probably given to the man of the house. The contrast – and nutrition of the poorest – is shocking. Which is why country-house servants believe they're more fortunate than most working-class people: they prepare and serve these vast mountains of food, so it follows that they too are fed each day – and sometimes quite well.

How is food cooked? Mostly on closed ranges, heated by coals, a labour-intensive method which is gradually being replaced by gas cookers – a quarter of families in towns and cities have a gas cooker by now. Yet most country-house kitchens continue to use the big range. And most of the food cooked in the below-stairs kitchen is consumed on the same or following day: domestic refrigeration is not yet commonplace, though ice from the ice chest is used for chilling fruit, wine and desserts as well as ice cream.

Here's a brief rundown on the food and the dishes the aristocratic family consume at home. Overall, the food is very rich, very tasty and beautifully presented. But there are no concessions to vegetarianism for those who don't eat meat – such beliefs are not fashionable and seen as eccentric or outlandish. And as we've already noted, the day's menu is presented by the chef or cook to the lady of the house each day for clearance. For special occasions, of course, these menus have to be planned well in advance. Yet food shopping itself isn't always on a huge scale: on a very big estate quite a lot of the produce is already available in-house, though certain foods are ordered from a local supplier. A saddle of mutton, for example, is ordered some days in advance from a local butcher.

Breakfast is a very substantial meal. And there are many dishes waiting on the overladen sideboard that we are familiar with today for the classic English breakfast: a battery of solid silver dishes containing porridge, bacon, sausages, eggs – fried, poached, or boiled – kidneys, smoked fish, grilled cutlets, kedgeree (see recipe below).

The breakfast menu also includes potted meats and pre-cooked dishes like curry, (India and the Raj are still very important to the aristocrats, curried eggs a big favourite), foods such as sardines on toast and big displays of cold meats like tongue, ham, even small quantities of game or roast fowls. At country-house shooting parties, breakfast for sportsmen may include game pie, devilled turkey and spiced beef. Piles of fruit are artfully displayed on sideboards, too. Plus toast, rolls, honey, marmalade, hot chocolate, coffee and tea.

The food is highly decorated, even at breakfast. If cold tongue, for instance, is on the menu, it is displayed in a special box-shaped holder. Like their houses, where the key idea is a specific room for a specific object or purpose, the wealthy Edwardians also use a range of kitchen and culinary equipment for table presentation that most of us would not recognise. The thick end of the tongue is placed in the holder and whipped butter is piped neatly along the top, complete with a sprig of parsley. Slices are carved from the thin end, as needed. Many dishes like this are then decorated with a white paper frill.

Lunch started to evolve as a meal in itself in the nineteenth century. Before it was merely a snack and 'dinner' was the day's main meal, taken in the middle of the day or the afternoon. But over time the main meal began to be taken later and later. So by the turn of the twentieth century – and with the introduction of artificial lighting – it became possible for society to partake of their main meal, dinner (not to be confused with 'supper' which is a very late meal, a snack of cold meats and cheese, served around 10pm), much later, at 8pm.

So by now, lunch is seen as a 'light' early afternoon meal. Yet it is still a three-course elaborate repast, served with wines and tea and coffee. Structurally, the idea is to start with a light dish, progress towards something heavier – like a meat course – then a final offering of something lighter.

HERE IS A FAIRLY TYPICAL LUNCH MENU:
- macaroni au gratin
- minced venison (croquettes made out of minced leftover venison, put into a sauce and seasoned)
- roast rabbit with potatoes, peas and carrots
- crème caramel or fruit compôte for dessert

Cold meats are also displayed on a sideboard as a buffet, so people can pick and choose. This is essentially a light meal. Popular dishes include mutton and fish like trout, salmon and crayfish, as well as whitebait, lobster mayonnaise (a very popular Edwardian dish), salmon, oysters, sole and langoustine. Turtle soup is also a favourite. Fish is often poached in an elaborate rich, creamy sauce. Or it is served in aspic (jelly) and garnished with herbs. And all fish is served boned.

Pâtés are also popular, usually sieved as highly as possible to ensure a velvet smooth texture. Anything with a soft texture like pâtés or soup is usually passed through a 'tammis' (a finely woven cloth) to make it super-smooth. Two kitchen maids hold the cloth, one at each end, and the soup is poured into the cloth, then it's pushed through with a spoon to ensure an ultra-smooth texture.

Soup itself is a fine art. And there's plenty of choice as Isabella Beeton, or Mrs Beeton as she is known, the author of the definitive and highly regarded housekeeping 'bible' of the nineteenth century, *Mrs Beeton's Book of Household Management*, points out:

> There are more than 500 different kinds of soup but they can be broadly divided into a few classes, namely broths, clear soups, thick soups and purées. The valuable dietetic properties of soup have been and indeed are much overlooked in this country. Yet no form of food is more digestible and wholesome, nor does any other method of preparing food afford so many opportunities for utilising material that would otherwise be wasted. The richness or quality of a soup depends more upon a proper choice of ingredients and an appropriate management of the fire in the combination of those ingredients, than upon the quantity of solid, nutritious matter employed: much more upon the art and skill of the cook than upon the sum laid out in the market. The average cook imagines that the goodness of soup depends upon the weight of meat she puts into it, and upon the size of the fire over which it is boiled.

Food Decoration is for 'special effect', everything must look good. Often, hot food is covered in a glaze (a heavily reduced veal stock) in order to make it shine. Other decorative touches used include anchovy fillets, fine green beans, cooked egg yolk (put through a sieve), or herbs like parsley and chervil.

Even cold dishes are surrounded by decorative effects: tiny bits of chopped aspic, carrots, potatoes, turnips 'turned' into small shapes or cold vegetables bound with mayonnaise to make Russian salad. An enormous amount of painstaking detail is involved in the presentation of the food – mostly it is the role of the cook or chef alone to create the final decorative effect – to ensure perfection.

Afternoon Tea is a ritual in itself. It is taken informally, in the drawing room, with all the cutlery placed on side tables. Although tea is primarily a feminine diversion, both sexes sometimes participate in the tea ritual. The ladies must wear their finest 'afternoon' clothing. Tea, Madeira cake, cherry scones, hot potato scones, flapjacks, coconut rocks, tiny cucumber sandwiches, cream, raspberry jam and butter – it's a social event, very much a way of filling in the hours before dinner so that local friends and relatives may exchange courtesies. If there are house guests during shooting parties, the array of teatime treats becomes even more extensive – lobster sandwiches, anyone? For house-party groups, it might even be taken outside, picnic style, in a specially erected tent, with wicker baskets of food and drink carried out, with due ceremony, by the servants.

Dinner is a very elaborate meal, a structured menu consisting of soup, entrée, fish, sorbet, then a roast, followed by dessert. Before dinner, the hostess must be ready in the drawing room, in her evening wear, at least fifteen minutes before the first guest arrives. Guests, in turn, know they are expected to be punctual.

When they arrive, they are ushered into the drawing room by the butler or first footman. For a dinner of more than six or eight people, each man is handed a place card carrying the name of the woman the hostess has placed next to him for dinner. If the man does not already know this woman, he must introduce himself and when the dinner gong sounds, he rises and offers her his arm. The dinner guests then move into the dining room, led by the host and the main female guest, the lady of the highest rank. This might be the eldest lady in the group or a stranger. But if there is a bride in the dinner group, precedence is given to her unless the dinner is being given specially for another female guest. Etiquette demands that husbands do not escort their wives into dinner – nor should brothers escort their sisters or sons escort their mothers. And the last couple in the dinner guest procession is the hostess, on the arm of the most socially important gentleman.

Invitations are issued to equal numbers of men and women, though it is sometimes appropriate to invite two or more 'extra' gentlemen – so that married ladies do not only have the option of going into dinner with each other's husbands.

At the dinner table, the host and the lady he has taken into dinner are seated at the bottom of the table, with the woman on the host's right hand. The hostess is seated at the top of the table and the gentleman who has accompanied her into dinner must sit on her left. At large dinner parties there will be place cards carrying the names of the guests on the table. Sometimes, the guest's name is printed onto a menu and positioned in front of each 'cover' (the name for the place laid at the table for each person). Menus are placed all along the dinner table, the dishes frequently written in French. Once a lady has taken her seat she may remove her gloves – long gloves can just be unbuttoned around the thumb and peeled back from the wrists.

WHICH CUTLERY?

Strict dining etiquette dictates which cutlery must be used:

- Soups are eaten with a tablespoon – always spooned away from the diner.
- Fish is eaten with a fish knife and fork.
- 'Made' dishes like rissoles and patties are eaten with a fork only.
- Poultry, game, asparagus, salads are eaten with a knife and fork.
- Peas are eaten with a fork.
- When eating game or poultry, diners must not touch the bone of either the wing or the leg with their knife.

- Sweets like jellies, blancmanges and puddings are eaten with a fork.
- Cheese is eaten very carefully. Small morsels are placed – with a knife – on small pieces of bread, brought to the mouth via thumb and finger.
- Grapes, cherries or pitted fruits are tricky: the pits and skins are spat discreetly into a hand and then placed on the side of the plate.
- Dessert is served to guests in the same order as dinner.

LEAVING THE TABLE

A lady wanting a second glass of wine must not help herself: the gentleman seated beside her must fill her glass. (The wine decanters are handed to the male guests only after the servants have left the dining room.) Around ten minutes after the wine has been passed round the table, it is the hostess who gives a signal for the ladies to leave the room, bowing to the lady of the highest rank. The gentlemen rise with the ladies, the women leave the dining room – in order of rank with the hostess last. Then the men are left to their port and claret, to smoke their cigars or cigarettes; the ladies move to the drawing room for coffee. The men join them later. Dinner ends officially about 30 minutes after this. However, in many country houses, the dinner group plays cards or bridge into the small hours.

THE MENU

Here's a dinner menu of six courses. (On special occasions there can be many more – between eight and twelve.):

- Caviar
- Fish soup
- Poached salmon with crayfish sauce
- Cutlets of pigeon

- Chicken Valencia with peas and creamed spinach
- Roast woodcock with peas and apricots

Other popular dishes include: Oyster Patties, Braised Celery, Roast Goose, Potato Scallops, Vanilla Soufflé.

Drinks at dinner include French wines, spirits, scotch whisky, sherry and port. They also drink hock, champagne, Sauternes and claret. (Non-alcoholic drinks served during the day include lemon barley water or, in summer, iced tea.)

Dessert is equally elaborate: blancmanges, hothouse fruit from the greenhouse, arranged in silver fruit dishes carefully lined with vine leaves, with the fruit built up in tiers. Often dessert fruit is arranged down the middle of the table amid the flower displays.

Jellies come in huge, fantastic moulds. A tall pillar jelly mould may be created with jellies of different colours, turned out so that each slice is presented in a multi-coloured pattern. A dinner table for twenty people may be decorated with up to a dozen ice-cream moulds in huge shapes.

FRENCH VERSUS RUSSIAN?

The preparation and presentation of food is complex enough, the table etiquette complicated, yet a younger, newly married and less experienced hostess might also face another small dilemma when planning a dinner party – deciding between two distinct styles of serving dinner:

- The fashionable *service à la russe* (Russian style). Here an array of different dishes are cut up on a sideboard, then handed round to the guests who take each dish as a course in itself. Or...
- The more traditional style, known as *service à la française*. This means the food is carved at the table and two large courses, each one including a variety of different dishes, are

placed on the table by servants, one after the other. This way, a dinner guest can help themselves and offer their neighbour dishes within reach – and ask for other dishes to be passed, either by another diner or by a footman.

According to the toffs' bible, *Etiquette: Rules & Usages of the Best Society*, this traditional style is more complex: 'A soup or fish course would have been on the table at the same time and would have been removed when the entrées (cutlets, fricassees, boudins, sweetbreads or pâtés) were served followed by the roast.'

The *Etiquette Rules* recommend the more fashionable (*à la russe*) style for the confused hostess: 'It gives an opportunity for more profuse ornamentation of the table, which, as the meal progresses, does not become encumbered with partially empty dishes and platters.'

As a consequence of all this, by 1914, the fashionable set have virtually abandoned the traditional style of presentation – but a hostess might still need to consider it when entertaining older relatives, like the fictional Dowager Duchess of Grantham, who still hankers for her mostly lost world of the 'old' ways.

Given the amount of food to be consumed at one sitting, you can't help wondering how the privileged women manage. They are beautifully clad yet tightly encased in stiff corsetry underneath, making movement extremely difficult. How do they cope with all this stuffing of the face? Put simply: with great difficulty. Fashionable women are expected to have a very small waist with curves above and below. (Very thin women don't become fashionable until after World War I.) Pecking at each course rather than tucking in with gusto is the only way to maintain a fashionable appearance and a degree of comfort. And, hopefully, keep the flab at bay.

WHAT DO THE SERVANTS EAT?

Though their food would sometimes consist of leftovers or fairly basic, plain food overall, the food the live-in country-house servants eat is, in many cases, quite good. In some big houses, the lady of the house gives the cook a written set of rules for amounts of food permitted for servant consumption each day, according to quantity or value. But quantity aside, much depends on the quality of the cooking; sometimes the cook will refuse to cook for the other servants. Then the kitchen maid has to do the best she can. So in some houses, servants' meals are heavily dependent on pre-cooked food (leftovers).

The uppers, of course, fare better food wise – particularly if they are in a house where they continue to eat separately from the lowers in their own quarters – dining off high-quality china and tableware. But overall, while the lowers' breakfast and break-time fare is very basic, the servants' main meal – the 'dinner' served around noon – is fairly substantial and very much 'meat 'n' two veg' type English food fare: stews (usually with cheaper cuts of meat) or offal or roast meat, often served cold (the leftover syndrome).

The vegetables, carrots, cabbage and potatoes on the table are plain, without elaborate sauces or garnish – but they're home-grown and fresh. The bread is not the sliced white or brown packaged variety we know but freshly baked from the kitchen; the butter is freshly churned, country style. Desserts are plain too, like rice pudding. But there's often cheese and seasonal fruit around: strawberries, raspberries, loganberries, peaches and apricots. And many houses permit a specific allowance of tea and sugar for their servants, so there are plentiful cuppas available, domestic tasks permitting.

At Longleat, Wiltshire, home to the Thynn dynasty, servant diaries during World War I record an abundance of game for their meals: pheasant, goose, venison, partridge, hare and rabbit, followed by cheese and puddings. Given the fact that the greater majority of the population are not, at any time, enjoying such fare, the advantages of working on a large, well-run estate, food wise at least, are clear.

But what do servants drink? The uppers drink wine with their meals but beer is the traditional servant drink and in previous centuries many country houses brewed their own. So they devised their own rules around beer consumption. These included small beer made available through the day (small beer is weak, with 2.5 per cent or less alcohol content) but stronger ale is strictly rationed – and sometimes only allowed on special occasions, like birthdays. (Men could drink double the amount that women were permitted to drink.) But after the nineteenth century, country houses start to buy in their alcoholic drinks and eventually abandon their own brewing. Cash is sometimes offered to servants in lieu of beer as part of the deal – 'beer money' – but servant alcohol abuse is often a problem – and alcohol abuse itself remains a huge social difficulty in Edwardian times, with thousands regularly prosecuted for drunkenness.

As a consequence, some country houses have very strict rules around alcohol and staff access to their vast wine cellars. Those whose work involves hanging around, waiting for their masters, especially in towns and cities where pubs are plentiful – and warm – are the most prone to alcohol problems: footmen, for example. Cooks and butlers are also prone to over-tippling or taking one-over-the-odds sometimes. Given the amounts of spirits and wine consumed by their masters, it's difficult to say how rigorous the toffs might be when it comes to monitoring the servants' intake. After a long day supervising the kitchen, is it so surprising that Cook might reach for the sherry bottle?

A DIET MAINLY CONSISTING OF BREAD

Between 1909 and 1913, a survey was conducted in Lambeth, South London, of a large group of working-class families, detailing how they fed, clothed and housed themselves on very low incomes. Conducted by Maud Pember Reeves and other members of the socialist Fabian Women's Group, the survey was published as a book, *Round About A Pound A Week*. This £1 (twenty shillings) was a standard wage then, a sum these families, often with several children, struggled to live on. The book's publication created a furore and was an important stepping stone in the ongoing campaign towards a fairer society and the welfare state. Here's what it says about the diet of these ordinary working Londoners:

> Without doubt the chief article of diet in a twenty shilling budget is bread. A long way after bread come potatoes, meat, and fish…potatoes are generally 2lbs for one penny, unless they are 'new' potatoes. Then they are dearer…
>
> Meat is bought for the men and the chief expenditure is made in preparation for Sunday's dinner, when the man is at home. It is eaten cold by him the next day.
>
> The children get a pound of meat 'pieces' stewed for them during the week…
>
> Bread, however, is their chief food. It is cheap; they like it; it comes into the house ready cooked: it is always at hand, and needs no plate and spoon. Spread with a scraping of butter, jam or margarine, according to the length of purse of the mother, they never tire of it as long as they are in their ordinary state of health. They receive it into their hands, and can please themselves as to where and how they eat it. It makes the sole article in the menu for two meals in the day. Dinner may consist of anything, from the joint on Sunday to boiled rice on Friday.

Potatoes will play a great part, as a rule, at dinner, but breakfast and tea will be bread.

THE UNHEALTHY EATERS

Both poverty and excess bring considerable health problems. The rich multi-course diet of wealthy Edwardians, the large amounts of meat, sugary foods washed down with sherry, hock, champagne or liqueurs leads to stomach and digestive illnesses. Diet-related health problems include jaundice, gallstones and gout. And for the poor, their limited diet and lack of knowledge about nutrition means malnutrition is widespread. At the time of the Boer War in 1899–1902, Army recruiters are shocked to discover that many would-be recruits are too undernourished to fight.

TEATIME

Here's a vivid description of a child's view of the Edwardian 'at home' afternoon tea ritual written by Constance Spry, a well-known writer of recipe books at the time.

These were dressy affairs in more ways than one. Tatted doilies, ribbon bound plate handles and tiered cake stands, impiously nicknamed 'curates', gave scope for competitive ingenuity – and a source of revenue for bazaars.

White kid gloves were de rigeur (a must). Woman's crowning glory was her hair, and she made the most of every bit of it. Glace silk petticoats swished, veils twisted themselves into knots no sailor would care to name, and immense feather boas framed the face in a seductive and feminine manner…whatever the hallowed day might be had a personality of its own; you could recognise it from the moment you came downstairs in the morning. The kitchen hummed with activity. The fire had to roar, the oven got hot, and was to be no nonsense on the part of anyone.

I have watched with unwavering concentration, miracles of sleight of hand. I have seen tightly gloved women balance a cup and saucer in the air, negotiate a knotted veil, and convey a tremulous cucumber sandwich from hand to mouth without a fault. Seldom have I had the satisfaction of seeing even a bit of tomato misfire.

The white gloves, in consideration of which the bread and butter had been rolled, might come to grief over hot buttery toast or too-soft sugar icing, but what of it? Such offerings on the altar of delicate behaviour only added lustre to a reputation of refinement.

Come Into the Garden, Cook by Constance Spry

ESCOFFIER

Often known as the 'king of chefs and chef of Kings' Georges Auguste Escoffier is a major figure in the development of modern French cuisine, earning a worldwide reputation as a director of the kitchens of the ultra-fashionable watering holes, the Grand Hotel, Monte Carlo and the Savoy Hotel in London. The gourmandizing Prince of Wales is a huge admirer of Escoffier and when he becomes King Edward in 1901, Escoffier is in charge of the banqueting for his Coronation. One of Escoffier's most famous dessert recipes, served in a silver bowl, is Pêche Melba (Peach Melba) in honour of Dame Nellie Melba, the Australian singer, a frequent guest at the Savoy. His cookbook, *Le Guide Culinaire*, published in 1903, continues to be a source of inspiration for chefs everywhere to this day.

PICNICS

The idea of dining outdoors started in the Victorian era. But with the introduction of the motorcar as transportation for food and picnic equipment, picnics became very popular in the summer months. Special picnic recipes evolve and new tableware is created to serve the potted cheese, potted pâtés, sandwiches and cakes that can now be enjoyed more readily outdoors.

BRANDED FOODS AND TAKEAWAYS

For the middle-class families with money to spend, commercially produced foodstuffs are starting to become more common by now. Things like baking powder, gelatine and tinned foods are readily available. In fact, many branded foods that are familiar to us now emerged in the Edwardian era. Brands and products like Marmite, Oxo, Birds Custard, Lyles Golden Syrup, Colman's Mustard, Heinz Ketchup, Typhoo Tea, Cadbury's Dairy Milk, and Perrier water are first launched at this time. There is even a very early version of Cup a Soup, called Edwards Dessicated Soup.

Street food, or takeaway food, is increasingly popular in London, particularly fish-and-chip shops or the more traditional pie shops, selling meat pies with mash and jellied eels (chopped eels in aspic).

SPOT THE NEW RICH

In a very grand house, families dine off gold and silver plate – the closet containing the plate often contains enough silver cutlery to serve hundreds of guests. In homes like Welbeck Abbey, the home to the Duke of Portland, the closet contains a complete cutlery service in gold to serve fifty people. Snobbish aristocrats know that one sure way to spot 'new' money at dinner parties is by looking at the cutlery. If the fish knives and forks match the rest of the cutlery, you are dining in a 'new money' house. How to tell? Ancestral silver never includes special cutlery for fish.

RECIPE FOR KEDGEREE

The origins of kedgeree go back to India: it became a popular breakfast dish in Victorian times – brought back from India by colonial administrators. It's the ideal leftover dish; it can be eaten hot or cold. Here's a simple recipe that will serve four people:

- 500g cooked, smoked haddock (cook by gently poaching the haddock in a saucepan for 10 minutes). When cooled, remove any skin or bones and flake the haddock gently into large pieces.
- 40g butter
- 1 large white onion finely chopped
- 500ml stock from the poached fish
- 200g washed basmati rice
- 1 teaspoon mild curry powder
- 2 tablespoons double cream
- 2 tablespoons chopped flat-leaf parsley
- 4 hard-boiled eggs, shelled and cut into quarters
- nutmeg and ground pepper

Method:

- Heat a small amount of the butter in a large frying pan. Gently cook the chopped onion.
- Heat the fish stock in a separate pan.
- Add the rice to the onion and stir well. Lower the heat. Sprinkle over the curry powder and mix well.
- Add fish stock and stir through. Bring to the boil, then simmer for ten minutes until rice is cooked.
- Stir in the remaining butter and cream. Add a pinch of ground pepper and a very small dash of nutmeg. Add the cooked fish and fold through the cooked rice.
- Then add the chopped parsley and finally the chopped eggs.

Recipe from chef, Miles Collins

RECIPE FOR HOT VANILLA SOUFFLÉ.
The soufflé is a very popular Edwardian dessert. Here's a simple recipe for four people:
- 25g butter
- 25g plain flour
- 150ml milk
- 25g caster sugar
- vanilla essence
- 4 eggs, separated

Method:
- Heat the oven to 200°C/Gas Mark 5.
- Prepare a thoroughly greased 150mm (6-inch) soufflé dish.
- Melt the butter in a saucepan and add the flour.
- Cook together gently for 1 minute.
- Gradually stir in the milk, beating constantly to ensure the sauce is smooth.
- Bring to the boil, stirring constantly.
- Remove from the heat and stir in the sugar and just a quarter of a teaspoonful of vanilla essence. Leave until the saucepan is cool enough to handle comfortably.
- Beat in the egg yolks, one at a time.
- Whisk the egg whites stiffly and fold carefully through the soufflé mixture.
- Turn into the prepared dish and bake in the centre of the oven for 30–40 minutes.
- Serve immediately.

From *The Book of Sweets & Puddings* by Myrtle Lindlaw

Longleat House.

Chapter 8

Entertainment & Sport

The dining rituals are one aspect of the intense social networking of the wealthy elite. Yet there are many other activities on the calendar that take up a great deal of their time – and create even more party planning for the servants and those working on the estate.

The traditional outdoor hunting, shooting, fishing lifestyle of the country house elite is long established. But as a means of lavishly funded social networking, its importance peaks in the Edwardian years, mainly because the country-house party featuring these upper-crust sporting pursuits has grown, mostly thanks to Edward VII's enthusiasm for all things related to pleasure and socialising, into a hedonistic, plush toff lifestyle – gracious living in a 'gilded age'.

THE SHOOTING PARTY

The weekend – or Saturday to Monday three-day country-house party – can sometimes extend to a party of two or three weeks duration, if it is held on one of the very big shooting estates like Blenheim Palace in Oxfordshire (home of the Churchill family), Chatsworth in Derbyshire, home to the 8th Duke of Devonshire and his wife Louise, or King Edward's own 8,000-hectare estate, Sandringham, in Norfolk, where his own railway station (at Wolferton) has been constructed, just two miles away from his hunting lodge, so that guests can arrive close to the estate for the big shooting parties.

Guests have their servants load up their car with an enormous leather trunk, containing enough outfits for five or six changes of clothing each day. Or the trunk is loaded onto a luggage van in a train, while the guests travel in the first-class compartments.

Shooting birds or game is very much the rich man's sport. Thousands of birds or 'bag' are shot in a three-day session hosted by the King for his tweed-suited guests, assisted by a large number of gamekeepers and estate workers (and sometimes locals hired for the purpose). It is, by today's standards, a very labour-intensive affair.

The gamekeepers have a big role to play in the planning of the shooting party. They work at rearing the game birds, protecting them from predatory poachers. They also have to make sure there are sufficient numbers available to shoot. As many as 20,000 pheasants, for instance, are bred in one year, all looked after by under-gamekeeping staff.

At the big shoot itself many other staff are involved: there are beaters – their role is to walk up from a certain point to drive the birds in the direction of the guns. There are loaders helping load the guns and cartridge boys helping, too. By tradition, the beaters wear white smocks, with large felt hats with wide brims, specially designed for safety reasons – and so that their visibility allows the head gamekeeper to keep an eye on their movements. Shooting itself is now much safer than in the previous century: breech-loading guns, copper percussion caps and self-contained central-firing cartridges mean more reliable firearms.

So great is the demand for, and popularity of, these high-maintenance shooting parties that cash-strapped landowners often rent out the rights to shoot, hunt and fish on their estates to the wealthy 'new money' entrepreneurs who haven't yet purchased their own.

Yet no matter how many birds the men, clad in their chunky tweeds, knickerbockers, thick stockings and heavy boots, may shoot, open boasting about exactly how many birds they've 'bagged' in one session is very much frowned upon: it's not the sort of thing a gentleman does. It's also considered uncivilised to discuss sport when ladies are present. Yet a gentleman does not stop to query the cost of a twelve-bore gun and leather case – around £150 at the time – three years' salary for a butler, shop or factory worker.

Around 30–40 guests at a time may be invited to these country-house parties to hunt, shoot and fish during the day and enjoy a number of different entertainments after dark. Card games and gambling are extremely popular after-dinner pursuits. Games like whist, backgammon and bezique, a French card game for two players, are also popular. Or they might play charades or other parlour games. But baccarat (an illegal card game much loved by the gambling-mad Prince of Wales) goes right out of fashion after 1891 when the Prince is involved in another huge scandal: one of his friends, Sir William Gordon Cumming, is caught cheating at the game and is rejected by society after a very public court case where he attempts to defend his reputation – and fails.

Baccarat is soon replaced with bridge, which becomes even more popular with women after the founding of fashionable ladies clubs in London in the late 1800s. Fancy dress parties are very much in vogue. Musical entertainments are organised. And, of course, the country-house party is the perfect opportunity to gossip, argue, flirt and more – in between indulging at the overladen dining table.

These house parties are not just about leisure and pleasure, of course. They are the elite's big opportunity to push forward their social and political ambitions. And, in the case of families with eligible grown-up children, this is the perfect chance to show them off to each other. In the most favourable light.

A beautiful young woman, attired in a figure-hugging riding habit with matching skirt atop a beautiful horse, ridden side-saddle with style and brio, has a powerful effect on admiring male eyes. Especially if breeding and inheritance are on the agenda.

While horse riding itself is popular with upper-crust women, they do not, as a rule, join the men at the shoot – it's not really considered conventional for women to do so. Nor is it correct etiquette. 'Ladies are better out of the way, unless they are very tractable and obediently follow close on the track of the sportsmen,' warns the aristos' etiquette bible, *Etiquette of Good Society*.

Yet shooting is such a major preoccupation that adept horsewomen, like Dame Mary Russell, Duchess of Bedford at Woburn Abbey in Bedfordshire, become crack shots, as well as riding in foxhunts, or riding to hounds, as it is known. Hunting the fox down in the woods is another aspect of the Edwardian country-house party that is very much taken for granted – as an upper-class sport, it does not create the controversy it does today. And it requires riding skill and stamina, chasing over hills, hedges and travelling long distances for a large part of the day. But nonetheless, the Edwardian elite horsewoman, with her small hard hat, long dark leather boots and looped riding skirt, experiences a rare sense of freedom and abandon as she gallops through the countryside. There is no rule which says the rider can't enjoy herself in the great outdoors.

There are many other diversions for the house-party guests. Huge lawns and gardens are laid out to promenade in. Guests can ride or walk through extensive parklands or take tea under an awning. Huge private libraries in the house offer a wide range of books or periodicals to browse through. Games of croquet and golf are popular with both sexes (in fact golf has become so well-liked by the early twentieth century that golfers are spending £4.7 million a year on the sport).

By now, many grand houses boast their own tennis court – sometimes more than one – and in the summer months, guests play tennis on the grass (hard courts are viewed as somewhat vulgar). As a sport, tennis is a late-Victorian innovation, so it is still very much a fashionable person's game. And, of course, another opportunity for a slender, beautiful young woman to show off her sporting prowess – and her shape – to the best advantage.

The outfits women wear to play all sports are very cumbersome, with long, heavy skirts (amazingly, some fashionable women go skiing in long skirts with breeches underneath: trousers for women do not appear until the twenties). Playing tennis in a clinging white skirt, dropping to just two inches above the ground, plus white blouse, white waistband and a light-coloured silk tie and white collar – doesn't seem like fun on a hot summer's day. And indeed, it is not unusual for sprained ankles to be a result of tripping over on a skirt hem. Yet for the highborn ladies, tennis is another fashionable pursuit – and women's fashion, by now, is gradually beginning to move away from the heavy restrictive clothing of the past.

If it rains, the guests might go for a ride. Sometimes a shopping expedition in the car is organised to a nearby town –

when the ladies are forced to cover their faces in long floaty veils because there's such a lot of dust flying around the bumpy country roads: protective goggles are also sometimes worn. And when the women return, to change, yet again, into their flimsy tea gowns before taking tea, the men take the opportunity to play billiards and snooker – playing these games after dinner is considered impolite and offensive to the women.

THE SOCIAL YEAR

In the nine years of his reign, Edward VII (or Edward the Caresser as history has dubbed him, because of the legion of mistresses he had following his marriage to Queen Alexandra in 1863) continues to pursue the high-maintenance country-house party lifestyle he'd created over many years as Prince of Wales, fitting it all in with his kingly duties which frequently take him on official trips abroad. Essentially, this highly social yet mainly sporting calendar goes like this:

August: Yacht racing on the Royal Yacht *Britannia* at Cowes, Isle of Wight. The King is a keen yachtsman. The last-ever royal racing yacht, the *Britannia*, built for him in 1893, is one of the most successful racing yachts in the world. And Cowes Week, organised by the exclusive Royal Yacht Squadron where class rather than cash is the entry point, is an ideal setting for the fashionable elite to show off – mostly to each other – against the backdrop of the yachts gliding along the Solent.

After the exhaustive social round of Cowes comes a stint at a German spa resort like Baden-Baden, Marienbad or Carlsbad, famous European spa centres where guests can fix digestive problems or ease ailments like arthritis by bathing in the warm thermal waters – or immersing themselves in mud. (These attempts at a more healthy spa 'cure' away from the excesses of the usual rich dining are somewhat tenuous: delicious menus still include calorie-laden delicacies like ices, sweetbreads or duck.) And another big attraction of Baden-Baden is its casino, a top draw for the wealthy gambler, as is Biarritz, where Edward loves to picnic alongside busy roads, pretending to be anonymous but knowing he is highly visible.

October: Deer-hunting in Scotland.

November Early spring is spent at the country-house estate – where the King, at Sandringham, frequently plays host to his rich cronies (dubbed the Marlborough House Set, after Marlborough House in London, his official residence when in town). Or his friends entertain him in their country homes (Queen Alexandra, discreet and tolerant of her husband's excesses, does not accompany him to these gatherings – which sometimes include the King's mistress of the time).

May: The focus is London and The Season again, after a month or so on the French Riviera in early spring. Attending the first night of the Opera Season at Covent Garden is an important 'see and be seen' event, a good opportunity for the women to show off their latest creations – and their jewels. Horse racing, too is another passion – and a costly one. The country-house set often organise house parties around the big summer race meetings at Newmarket, Ascot, Sandown, Goodwood and Epsom where the women display their fashionable outfits and the men frequently race their own horses – and blow huge sums of money on equestrian betting and gambling.

Theatre-going, as well as opera, forms part of the social calendar, in the opulent surroundings of the new, plushly decorated grand theatres of the West End of London. Formal evening dress is worn for opera and theatre-going, though the upper crust audience do not expect – or get – anything too daring or controversial up on the stage; the fashionable set expect to be dazzled by spectacularly beautiful sets rather than thought-provoking drama.

Wimbledon in **June** is another sporting highlight as are the big dates on the cricket calendar: the April openings at the Oval and the July Test Matches at Lord's are all occasions where the elite indulge endlessly in the Good Life – and keep a close eye on each other's doings.

And so it goes on, an endless round of parties, balls, weddings, race meetings – and servant management. For the mistress of the country or town house, the organisation of such an intensely social round of activity is both time-consuming and exhausting. Given the dictates of The Season and the exclusivity of the elite circle, many guests visit the same houses, year after year, a tight, jewel-encrusted coterie of people locked into a world of glittering displays of ostentation and wealth.

There are certain drawbacks: if the house party includes King Edward VII, getting to bed after a long day can be tricky and often means a very late night given his dedication to food, wine and life's pleasures. Royal etiquette demands that no lady retire before the Queen – who mostly doesn't attend the house parties – and no gentleman can climb into his bed until the King decides to spread his huge bulk between the sheets of the regal boudoir.

The King must travel with two valets to keep him looking slick and spruce at all times, as well as half a dozen other servants, his private secretary and two equerries. He has a somewhat disconcerting habit, when hosting a shooting party at Sandringham, of having all the clocks in the house set forward by half an hour – to give him more time for hunting. And if he is a guest at one of his set's country houses, the hostess must always remember his bedside requirements: a cold roast chicken by the bed, in case he fancies a snack in the small hours.

Being part of this elite group means that the royal tastes eventually dictate the habits of everyone else; at one point, the traditional after-dinner ritual of cigars for the men is changed by the King to include cigarettes. And eventually it becomes more fashionable for women to smoke. This means special orders for the butler and the staff – because the traditional after-dinner serving of port has to be replaced with brandy, since brandy and cigarettes are seen to complement each other. Attention to detail at all times, 24/7.

In view of all this, the make-up of the country-house shooting party is very carefully considered: the names of the guests are carefully listed in the social columns of the London newspapers. (Etiquette dictates that such guest lists are made up of people who know each other, anyway.) So the indoor staff, especially the butler, housekeeper and cook, spend a great deal of time, in between their everyday duties, making sure that everything goes exactly to plan. Guests may bring their own personal servants too, so there is a lot of communication between staff from other great houses – and usually a lot of gossip, too. Not surprisingly, given the boredom of the rigid social routine, the country-house party is also the prime opportunity for the wealthy guests to indulge in extra marital dalliance (see Chapter 10 for more on this).

The lady of the house, in planning the event, must use incredible tact and discretion when considering the needs of her guests. In order to amuse or entertain the wives while the husbands are off shooting, for instance, she will sometimes invite a few spare men who don't care for sport to make light, even flirtatious conversation or gossip with the women. (These are called 'lap dogs', which gives a pretty clear idea of their role.)

And when it comes to drawing up the sleeping arrangements she has to be very cautious, too. The rules dictate that the name of each guest is written on a card, which is then slipped into a tiny brass frame on the bedroom door. But whose name should be displayed on the card of the room next door? It can be very tricky. A man who considers himself a great lover of women can get quite upset if his next door neighbour is a woman accompanied by her husband. And so on…

ENTERTAINMENT FOR THE SERVANTS

While their limited time off (half a day a week and one day off a month) and brief holiday periods are in stark contrast to the endless leisure pursuits of their masters, the servants do get to enjoy their time off, although a relatively isolated country house can't offer the same diversions for relaxing pursuits as those found in the town or city.

In the very big, grand country houses, the large numbers of servants working there often form a little community among themselves, especially if the lower servants' relationships with each other are friendly.

In the evening, between chores, they might read a newspaper, play dominoes or cards. Or sing, accompanied by a piano-playing colleague who enjoys tinkling the keys of the servants' hall piano in the corner. Making music is a cheerful diversion; someone might play a banjo, or a fiddle. It's a time for housemaids to chatter, exchange thoughts, as they work on their sewing – away from the stern gaze of the housekeeper or the unwanted leering of a new, lecherous second footman.

In the daytime, walking is the most common way of enjoying time off, given the complete lack of alternatives in the countryside. It's healthy, at least. Footmen, chosen for their physical attributes, are traditionally the fittest, most athletic of the country-house staff. A footman might walk several miles during his time off. Some employers even encourage footmen to keep fit by rowing on a lake on the estate. The housemaid on her day off is most likely to take a walk through the country lanes with other servant girls in the area or perhaps take tea with them. Bicycles, at this time, have become safer, cheaper and more commonplace. So the use of a bike, if it's available, can make a big difference to precious time off; it makes it easier, for instance, to cycle into the nearest town.

Church every Sunday, which the servants attend with the family, the lowers walking the two or three miles and back while the uppers and family are transported by horse-drawn trap or car, isn't exactly entertainment as such. But it does afford the opportunity to be sociable and exchange pleasantries with other workers in the area; given the size of the house and estate, there are always casual workers, carpenters and artisans working around the house to chat to briefly during the day. Friendships are most likely to be formed, however, between female lower servants. We're still a long way off from male/female platonic friendship in this segregated environment.

A servant's one-week annual holiday is mostly spent visiting family. And this must be arranged with the housekeeper to fit in with the routine of the house. Quite often, the holiday break is taken when the family is away in London during The Season and the big spring-cleaning session is being organised in the house. Which doesn't allow much of a break from the daily grind. Especially when you consider that going home, for female servants, often means cleaning or cooking if there are younger siblings or older relatives at home.

But servant socialising isn't always as limited as we might imagine. The valets and lady's maids travel with the job, all over the country, to London and abroad. It's a chance to experience very different environments, some of them scenically stunning, some exciting – think the South of France or Derby Day – or very grand settings like the poshest town houses in the London Season. Mostly, they're working. And they might have to sleep in the smallest or lowliest room in the house. But the experience itself in different surroundings is stimulating, and there are always other servants around, working for other families, to network with.

THE OFFICE PARTY

In some country houses, the toffs encourage the servants and estate staff to organise their own entertainment, with regular staff dances every month in the servants' hall. If the outdoor staff joins in, there are no shortages of male partners for the housemaids to dance with. Or flirt with (discreetly). And a celebratory tenants' dinner is traditionally thrown by the bosses if a new male heir is born, simultaneously raising employment hopes on the estate, a job in the baby's nursery, for example, or as a wet nurse.

Mostly, though, the bosses organise formal once-a-year staff dances for the servants which they attend as benevolent masters. Everyone has to dress up. It's a big date on the calendar – though in some houses, where servant-master relationships are not exactly warm, they're viewed with a mixture of anticipation and scepticism, similar to the feelings we sometimes have about annual office parties, if you like. If you don't like the boss and his missus, how can you fully relax when they're around?

It's even harder to relax and let your hair down if your working life is controlled by so many different rules and regulations. These big formal occasions are thrown open to everyone on the estate; the tenants, their families, even local tradesmen are invited by the toffs – and everyone wears their best party or ball dresses to enjoy the food and drink and perhaps dance the night away. Whatever their feelings about the bosses or the uppers, most have a good time. And there's bound to be plenty of fodder for gossip the next day.

PRESENTS FOR THE SERVANTS

The other big day on the calendar, of course, is Christmas. This is usually celebrated by a huge dinner in the servants' hall for all the indoor and outdoor servants. The hall is decked with bows of holly and there is a generous supply of punch, ale and beer to wash down the splendid meal: a roast, usually beef, with Yorkshire pudding and all the trimmings followed by plum pudding and mince pies. Later, according to the custom of the family who usually organise a gift-giving session with the servants after they've exchanged gifts with each other, the servants line up – in their usual pecking order of seniority – to be handed their Christmas gifts.

Like everything else, the giving of Christmas presents to servants is carefully planned. Housekeepers are in charge of organising and sourcing the gifts – and keeping a detailed record of the costs for their bosses. And the gifts themselves tend to be given strictly in accordance with the status of the servants.

As usual, the men do much better than the women, especially the uppers – a valet or male chef could be the recipient of a handsome present like a Gladstone bag costing three guineas (three pounds and three shillings). Or a head gardener would be given an easy chair of the same value. A first footman might receive a cash gift, as much as £5 if the boss is generous, but ten shillings is more common for a gardener or a housemaid.

Giving gifts of clothing to lower servants is something of an obsession with some country-house bosses, a practical but not very popular – or generous – gift. A lower maid might receive a length of cloth, either black for Sunday or flowered cotton for day wear (to be made up at her own expense) for work-wear. A housemaid is given a petticoat; an under lady's maid gets a black dress – to work in. As for the female uppers, they too get somewhat practical three-guinea gifts: a black silk dress for the housekeeper and an umbrella and handbag for the lady's maid.

Sometimes the children of the house are deployed to do the honours, to go down the line of servants, handing each their gift in turn and wishing them a happy Christmas, while the servants try to show gratitude. This is a charming gesture, especially if the children are quite small – and it's likely the servants will have formed some sort of relationship with the children who run around the kitchen area. But the truth is, anyone who has been working in the household for a few years knows exactly what to expect: yet another reminder of their status and how their employers, mostly, see them in work terms, rather than individuals whose personal qualities are to be valued. It's a once-a-year opportunity to garner goodwill from those who serve them, to show the staff some genuine appreciation. But it's usually a missed opportunity which becomes, as usual, yet another formality. Another day, another ritual. 'Twas ever thus...

HANDS OFF, YOU POACHERS

In 1911, so great is the need to employ gamekeepers on country estates, to protect the birds from poachers, that rural areas are employing twice as many gamekeepers as policemen.

LAST WORDS OF A SPORTING KING

On his deathbed in 1910 the King is informed that his horse, Witch of the Air, has won a race at Kempton Park. 'I am very glad,' says the King, his last words. Not long after he lapses into a coma and dies.

A FLYING SHOT

Woburn Abbey's Dame Mary Russell, Duchess of Bedford, is a keen horsewoman and bird watcher as well as a crack shot when shooting game. In 1918 she finances and built several hospitals in the Woburn area; in the thirties she works as a nurse. She later develops a passion for aviation, flying solo to South Africa in 1930. She dies in 1937, aged 71, when her plane crashes into the North Sea.

'I THOUGHT I WAS WINNING'

The 5th Earl of Rosslyn, James Erskine, is a war correspondent, actor and legendary gambler. He is also the half brother of the famous royal mistress, Daisy, Countess of Warwick. The Earl inherits £50,000 and an annual income of £17,000 with his titles, as well as an estate of over 3,000 acres – but is eventually declared bankrupt, later admitting that he has squandered his inheritance on horse-racing and cards. 'I can't understand it: I always seemed to be winning,' he says at the time.

As a bankrupt he is unable to take his seat in the House of Lords. Married three times – his second wife, US beauty Anna Robinson, is forced to pay his gambling debts during their two-year marriage – though the incorrigible Earl claims that after two days of marriage they never saw each other again.

LADIES CLUBS

London clubs catering only to women of rank and means – and mirroring the exclusive gentlemen's clubs of Pall Mall, like White's or Boodle's – become centres of leisure and relaxation for country-house ladies. These clubs have dining rooms, reading rooms and card rooms where wealthy women can play bridge and socialise with each other, far from the cares of country-house life. Many become addicted to playing bridge for large sums of money. Their exclusivity is demonstrated by the rules of the very first Ladies' Club in London, the Alexandra. Prospective members must be eligible to attend the Drawing Rooms – of the Court of the Queen.

BIKING FOR EVERYONE

By the 1890s 'safety' cycles started to take over from the older penny-farthing bikes, and soon prices of bikes are within the reach of ordinary working people.

Second-hand bikes cost around £2. Or a brand new bike can be purchased (on an instalment plan) for around £10. Cycling to get around then becomes available to both sexes, all ages, which is a huge leap forward for everyone.

OH WHAT A NIGHT...

The Servants' Ball is a significant date on the rural events calendar. Here's an extract from a local newspaper report in Fochabers (near Elgin, Moray, Scotland) for 6 November 1913.

The Annual Ball given by the 7th Duke of Richmond and Gordon for the servants in the castle, gamekeepers, ghillies, gardeners, estate employees also shopkeepers and tradespeople of Fochabers and neighbourhood took place on Friday night.

The ball was held in the magnificent dining room of the castle, transformed for the evening into a ballroom. In every way the assembly proved a brilliant success. Music was supplied by Barr Cochrane's band from Elgin, while Pipe Major McKenzie, the Duke's piper, played for the Highland dances. The Duke opened the ball in person, leading off the Grand March with Mrs Dallas, Housekeeper...

Supper was served at midnight and a lengthy toast list gone through with the health of the host and family being proposed by the House Steward, Mr. Compton.

Although the ducal family retired before supper, dancing was resumed and kept up until an early hour.

Chapter 9

Getting Around

It's September. A steam train is slowly making its way from Nottingham to Helmsdale, in the Scottish Highlands where the 6th Duke of Portland and his family are heading for the shooting season. The journey takes fourteen hours. But this is a special train: it has four carriages, a caravan of wealth and privilege. Inside the big first carriage – which includes bedrooms, a sitting room and a dining room – sit the owners of Welbeck Abbey, the 6th Duke and Duchess of Portland. In the next carriage, their children William, Francis and Victoria are being supervised by their governess. Inside the third carriage, footmen, the chef, the family's chauffeurs and the personal servants so necessary to the needs of their masters all travel together. And, true to the rules and strict hierarchy, the fourth passenger car carries the lower servants – the housemaids, kitchen or stillroom maids. The rest of the train is made up of a chain of wagons, each one carrying an automobile. The Portlands are on the move...

Dinner is due to be served to the family by railway staff. The servants are about to tuck in too, although their food comes out of the big wicker baskets they've brought with them: sandwiches, fruit, chicken and eggs, packed by the staff at Welbeck Abbey who are already busy with the major spring-cleaning session the housekeeper has organised in the family's absence. There is even a little stove and a teapot, for the uppers to make their own tea.

This is Toff Travel, Edwardian style. It beats Ryanair. Even if it is slow. Everything they need goes with them. Even if there are other helpers available – and there will be plenty of other servants around when they reach their destination – having their own 'team' to hand isn't seen as an indulgence. Nor is transporting all their motorcars across the country. It's just necessary to their way of life.

Luxury travel by train or boat is commonplace for aristocrats on the move. Only first-class plane travel is still ahead: the first successful plane flight in England takes place in 1900 and while progress in aviation is made in the following years, flying doesn't become a fashionable means of upper-crust travel until much later.

CARS & TRAINS

For the super-rich, getting around, at home or abroad, is more exciting than it ever was: the novelty of the motorcar means that the old horse-drawn cabs or carriages that dominated road transport in the previous century are vanishing. King Edward VII is the first British monarch to own a car, a Daimler Phaeton, purchased in 1900. Four years later, car registration is introduced and there are 8,500 cars on British roads. The first ever Rolls-Royce, the epitome of Edwardian style and luxury is unveiled in 1906.

Owning a car is only the province of the wealthy and privileged. But it's making a huge difference to the way they live: another good reason why the 'Saturday to Monday' country-house party has become so important: the toffs can now use the chauffeur to drive them there. And the early need for a man to walk and wave a red flag in front of every car on the road has gone. (The Red Flag Act, introduced in mid-Victorian times but withdrawn in 1896, stipulated that all mechanically powered road vehicles must be preceded by a man on foot, waving a red flag to warn the public.) However, this new, exciting innovation has its drawbacks: not all cars have windscreens. And sometimes their engines just… blow up. Or the tyres explode.

There are 303 people involved in fatal accidents involving the new motorcars in London in 1909 (with 3,488 accidents recorded) yet nothing can diminish the wealthy person's enthusiasm for the motorcar. The switch to motorised vehicles, of course, means staffing changes in some of the country estates; the new chauffeurs are often resented by existing staff – or seen as being a bit too 'above themselves', as indeed some are. But the march of progress is relentless: in their travels between town and country, the motorcar, for short journeys, is now becoming essential to the upper crust way of life. And toffs in London now have motorised cabs or taxis which they can hail to take them to and from parliament or their club.

For longer journeys, Britain's cross-country railway infrastructure is thriving; the very first restaurant cars have been introduced (on the Great Northern line) in 1879, and these start out as luxurious dining options: the kitchens fitted with coke-burning ranges and a scullery boy to peel potatoes and perform other menial chores on an open platform at the rear of the train. Heating's initially a bit of a problem: early foot warmers are merely oblong boxes filled with hot water, until steam heating is introduced. Yet despite some initial upper-class disapproval when it becomes obvious that railways will give people of all classes greater mobility, by 1900 trains are a way of life for millions. And a complete underground circuit linking the whole of London has already been established by that year: all the more reason for the wealthy, class-bound toffs to travel around in their motorcars or stay cocooned on a train in their 'bubble' of extreme luxury; rubbing shoulders while travelling with the rest of the population is unthinkable.

LIFE AT SEA

The travelling toffs can now also take advantage of the huge progress in maritime engineering and shipbuilding: this is the era of the great ocean liner, capable of crossing the Atlantic in a matter of days – and these huge first-class liners are designed specially for the super-rich, usually the wealthy new money industrialists heading for New York and the New World on a business trip.

The ill-fated *Titanic* is one of these luxury liners, launched by the White Star Line, in direct competition with Cunard, who launch the *Mauretania* and *Lusitania* in 1907, the first ever ocean liners to give birth to the phrase 'floating palace'. Until then, a trip across the Atlantic involved travelling on an early version of a Cross Channel Ferry – not very desirable for those who prefer to travel in luxury and style.

The trip across the Atlantic on one of these new luxury liners is faster too, taking between five and seven days. And everything about these ships has been created with the wealthy passenger in mind. The *Mauretania*'s interiors are designed by the same design duo (Mewes and Davis) who have created the sumptuous interiors for the Ritz Hotel: the idea is to make their first-class customers believe they are 'at home' in an environment resembling a grand hotel like the Ritz, which opened in 1906; it was the King's favourite haunt and built to resemble a stylish block of Parisian flats. Complete with Escoffier cuisine.

These trips are incredibly expensive. A first-class passage, Southampton to New York, costs the equivalent of the price of an expensive car nowadays, around £20–£30,000 return. And when it comes to the comfort of their pampered guests, no luxury is left out by the designers simply because these ships are designed for the new money no object, 'go for it' entrepreneurs, captains of industry whose millions are made in commodities or raw materials. But of course, the old money aristos must travel this way too, to keep up in the style stakes – even if it does go against the grain for them to rub shoulders with the untitled new money, they'll now grit their teeth and join them at the dinner table.

The interiors of the public rooms are very much in the style of the era: lots of polished wood, stained glass and gleaming brass fittings. Thick Turkey carpets, huge tapestries, enormous oil paintings, very rich furnishings – and elaborate fireplaces with electric fires. The *Mauretania* is among the first of the ocean liners fitted with electric lighting. The doomed *Titanic*, which sets sail a few years later, is also one of the new-style electrically-lit liners. Mains electricity is not installed across the UK until after World War I, so this is state-of-the-art innovation. In the bedrooms, there are plug-in electric reading lights by the beds, hyper-luxury – most of the British toffs haven't yet got round to installing such things at home.

Everything on board ship shrieks luxury and sumptuous living. Liners like the *Olympic*, *Titanic* and *Britannic* boast four 'parlour' suites in first class, though the name belies the size: each suite contains a private sitting room, two bedrooms and a private bathroom. All are sumptuously furnished and the cabins have portholes. Yet such is the desire of the designers to give their first-class travellers a consistent illusion that they are not, in fact, crossing the grey choppy Atlantic waters but are 'at home' wallowing in the luxury that is their natural habitat, that all the portholes are disguised – with an inner bay of pretty stained glass. This way, it looks like a very grand hotel.

The twelve other first-class suites each have a private bathroom and two rooms. And the toffs' personal servants, the lady's maid and valet, are accommodated nearby – on the other side of the corridor, opposite the first-class cabins. The servant's cabins don't have portholes or bathrooms; they can use the communal bathrooms nearby. And, of course, the servants must dine in their own quarters; they have a separate dining area on a nearby deck. Technically, the personal servants are travelling first class, but in reality, their accommodation is a cramped, dark room without facilities – just feet away from their lords and masters.

These liners boast two enormous restaurants for their super-rich travellers. There's a tiny smoking room, a modest-sized lounge and a ladies' card room, but the core of the first-class public space is the vast restaurant area. Given that life on board revolves around the restaurants, every aspect of the toffs' dining experience is perfectly considered. For instance, the super-rich like to see themselves as trend setters – so the Olympic liner has a first-class restaurant with dining tables for four – or even two. This is very new; the traditional dining style is for long tables with everyone in a row. But the designers of the Olympic liner have put in the small tables specially to attract the monied classes travelling for business: it's easier to talk business this way.

We might think such minor matters as table size are irrelevant. Yet to the toffs, whose attention to detail in all they do is consistent and heavily focused on etiquette, such things are important talking points: social snobbery taken, as usual, to an extreme.

Life on board the liners revolves around the restaurants. In the morning, after dressing and a substantial breakfast, couples might take a promenade around the first-class section – the luxury parlour suites also have their own private area to promenade in – then recline briefly on the plush sofa in their cabin, change clothes and glide in to lunch. Then the men step out for a smoke, the women might try a hand of cards, maybe another turn around the private deck for the air – and then head back to the cabin to change into quite elaborate evening gear for dinner, helped by the lady's maid. Their routine remains as it is at home: making several changes of clothes throughout the day, taking the air – and eating enormous meals.

So much fine attention is given to the smallest detail that the designers of the ocean liners even have special items made just for their rich passengers: an equivalent of today's hotel bathrobe, or the basket of posh toiletries in the bathroom. Only they're a bit more upmarket: consider a caviar dish, including a special ice compartment, specially made, in limited numbers, for the ship's first-class passengers. Or a special brass duck press. Everything is top-notch, finest quality, tailored to this exclusive and very wealthy market for whom money is no object.

WHAT DO THEY EAT?

Here's an example of what is prepared by the ship's, mostly French, kitchen staff for an eleven-course dinner on the *Titanic* – before disaster strikes:

- Hors d'oeuvres
- Oysters
- Consommé Olga
- Cream of Barley

- Salmon, Mousselline Sauce, Cucumber
- Filet Mignons Lili
- Saute of Chicken Lyonnaise
- Vegetable Marrow Farcie
- Lamb & Mint Sauce
- Roast Duckling & Apple Sauce
- Sirloin of Beef
- Chateau Potatoes
- Green Peas
- Creamed Carrots
- Boiled Rice
- Parmentier & Boiled new potatoes
- Punch Romaine
- Roast Squib & Cress
- Cold Asparagus Vinaigrette
- Pâté de Foie Gras
- Celery
- Waldorf Pudding

The servants eat much plainer fare on board, prepared in the ship's enormous galley kitchen where separate designated teams of cooks prepare food for the officers, ship's staff and the three different classes of passengers on board. It may be largely of the 'meat and two veg' variety they eat normally, but it's plentiful enough and quite nutritious.

Not all servants travel first class: rich families travelling with a servant retinue often fork out for their personal servants or children's nurses to travel first class (so they can have them to hand at all times), but the cooks, chauffeurs and lower servants travel in second or third class. So for a young person in service, this kind of luxury leisure travel is an experience in itself, certainly. But given their status, their time on board is still very much business as usual. And if they're travelling to stay with very wealthy American families in their huge mansions, there will be other servants there, too – although their bosses will have slightly less rigid or formal views about those who serve them.

HOW THE SERVANTS GET AROUND

As we've seen, using a bike or going on foot is still the primary means of getting around for country-house servants when they're not working. Yet they need to be careful when negotiating the road – fines for cycling without lights, for instance, are as much as five shillings, plus five shillings expenses, in 1913. Motorised bikes too are starting to appear – Triumph start mass production in 1903 – but these, of course are way out of reach, pricewise, for most.

Yet public transport is changing, especially in the cities, giving millions of working people the chance to get around locally: railway services are now being extended to the newer suburbs, built to meet the housing demands of the rapidly growing population and the increasing numbers of shop and office-bound staff. These suburban rail lines are very much for working people to use and their development widens many employment opportunities that hadn't existed before.

In or around a big city, for instance, servants who opt not to live in can, in some instances, now work closer to home if they can afford the suburban commuting fares. Everyday lives are being transformed – because it's now so much easier to get around.

In cities, commercial deliveries continue to be by horse and cart. But people are using a number of other road travel options: horse-drawn tram, motorised tram or even trolley bus. The trams run on tracks set into the road but they are hazardous; the drivers can't steer them properly and other road users need to keep a constant eye out for them. Cyclists, in particular, are wary of the tramlines because their wheels can easily get caught in the channels on either side of the rails, unless the cyclist rides across rather than along them. Tram networks are expensive to set up, so they do not run everywhere.

Trolley buses are better – they make contact with overhead cables for their power. Yet the open tops of some of these forms of transport mean that in windy or wet winter months they're not particularly pleasant, although waterproof covers for top-deck passengers are thoughtfully provided, attached to the seat in front. (Covered top buses, trams and trolley buses don't start to emerge until after World War I.) Servants had to pay varying amounts for their travel:

- A local tram ride, in 1906 in Dartford, Kent, costs one penny (a halfpenny is the special 'working man's fare').
- Train fares are more costly, even for those who can only afford to travel third class. In 1911, a 32km (or 20-mile) journey between Scarborough and Pickering takes 1 hour and 10 minutes, and the return third-class fare is 1 shilling.
- A cheap weekday return suburban train fare, Plumstead in South London to Charing Cross, costs 4 pence in 1903.

There is another travel option, widely available since the railways were developed in Victorian times: the network of coastal steamer services along the coastline of the UK; these companies now compete heavily with each other to persuade people to make short sea ferry rides, often in conjunction with the railway companies. And the improved design of British packet steamers – the first turbine-powered steamer, the *King Edward*, sets sail in 1901 – provides a much more efficient use of steam power for these short journeys and offers a useful travel alternative for anyone wanting to visit family living in a coastal area.

This kind of service is very popular in remoter areas like

Scotland; many are run as part-rail, part-steamer services. But the cost is still high on a servant's pay: a third-class fare on a part rail, part steamer run from Aberdeen to Oban costs 27 shillings. For a housemaid, earning £30 a year and hoping to send money home to help support her family, it means saving hard for maybe two years. And having to be content with letter-writing in the meantime.

Though a week's holiday by the seaside is way out of reach financially, two city servants with a day off together might take a special day-trip excursion train to enjoy a few hours at the seaside – or travel to another big city for an outing, to see the sights. And some country-house employers do give their staff time off for good work completed. So even a half day off can be enjoyed in this way.

There is another important angle to all this greater mobility: a servant unhappy in their job and wanting to move on can, in their time off, travel to the big city to job hunt: big city employment agencies are thriving, because the demand for good servants remains high among the middle classes. So if they have the requisite 'character' then time off can be used this way, especially in free-spending places like London where the new luxury palace-type hotels, like the Savoy in the Strand, are keen to recruit experienced servants with good characters who have already worked for the upper crust and understand their whims and fancies.

Personal servants, of course, get a taste of such grand hotels, here and abroad, when they accompany their employers at certain times of the year. It's a logical step for an ambitious servant to consider such steps up towards a live-out role: a head waiter, for instance, working at the Savoy can boast of take-home pay, mostly made up of very generous tips, at as much as £100 a week. Loyalty to the master versus that kind of pay? No contest.

Cities, of course, offer a lot of fun, even for those on low wages. There are parks and pleasure gardens, some with free entertainment. Music halls with big variety acts are also a great diversion for the footloose footman on a day off. And cinemas are starting to open up, too. At first, the music halls start to bring moving picture screens into their theatres. Then, between 1909 and 1914, many new cinemas open up all over the country. Pricewise, they are aimed at the masses: two or three pence will buy a cheap seat – but people can pay as much as two shillings for a reserved leather tip-up seat in a brand new cinema to watch short films, like *Pathé News*, followed by a love story or a comedy. The entire programme lasts about an hour. And the popularity of the new 'moving pictures' is such that their masters are indulging in their own movie shows: the well-heeled can now buy their own projectors and acquire what we'd call 'soft porn' movies to entertain their friends.

But it is Britain's seaside resorts that have really established themselves with ordinary working people now that millions can get there by train. Hundreds of seaside towns all over the country have gradually been transformed into places where working people can enjoy themselves, not just on the beach or in the sea – bathing machines, established by the Victorians in order to segregate the sexes are, by now, becoming extinct though they don't disappear from Britain's beaches until 1914 – but by strolling around the huge pleasure piers, pavilions and bandstands, or spending time in seaside gardens, music halls and theatres. This is outdoor leisure on a grand scale for everyone, much of it developed via the success of the railway companies – and sometimes helped by funds from wealthy aristocrats like the Duke of Devonshire who pours money into Buxton Spa, close to his Derbyshire home, Chatsworth House.

By 1911, 55 per cent of the British population spend at least one day at the seaside in the summer. Paid holidays, longer than just half a day, are now being introduced into the general workplace, so even those with little money can now enjoy the freedoms of nature; sunshine, beach and water together, if they can afford the 3d (threepence) for a deckchair.

There is, of course, a hierarchy of seaside resorts. Some, like Southport, start out catering to the monied classes but eventually, given the huge popularity of the resort, cater increasingly to the masses. Margate in Kent is very much aimed at the lower end of the market, its piers, like many round the country, offering men a penny-a-peep at the Mutoscope machine. A turn of the handle reveals a series of jerky images stuck onto a card of a woman taking off her clothes. No such machine exists at nearby Broadstairs, however, which is more expensive and only for the discerning, with its literary connection with Charles Dickens, who lived there at one stage. And so it goes on. Blackpool and Skegness? Too common for the posh middle classes.

But even if it's only affordable for a few hours, servants are now, for the first time in their history, able to enjoy themselves away from the constraints of their environment. Ordinary people are now starting, albeit on a small scale, to be consumers. Is it so surprising, then, that young girls getting a glimpse of all this, no matter how brief, are no longer so happy to put up with the long hours and constraints of going into service that their ancestors accepted as their lot?

THE PASSPORT

Passports are not required for international travel until 1914. Originally valid for two years, they carry a personal description section, like 'shape of face', 'complexion' and 'features', which is a bit too much information for some.

Being described as having a broad forehead, a large nose and small eyes upsets people. They think it's 'dehumanising'.

THE DUCK PRESS

The Edwardians love glazes, shiny surfaces on their food. And a duck press to create such a glaze is a necessity when serving pressed duck. Here's how it works: the breast and leg are removed from the roasted duck. The brass contraption has a press handle, which the chef or cook can rotate clockwise to extract the juice and marrow out of the remaining duck bones. This is then added to wine, brandy and seasoning to make a glaze or sauce for the accompanying duck meat.

'NO TRAINS THANKS, PEOPLE MIGHT USE THEM'

The 1st Duke of Wellington – who oversaw the Battle of Waterloo – worries that the railways might encourage poor people to go to London. Even worse, he fears that trains coming from Bath or Bristol would pass the toffs' hallowed educational establishment, Eton, and the noise – and they were pretty noisy then – might disturb the pupils.

CABBIE!

The horse-drawn two-seat, two-wheel carriages called 'cabriolets' found on city streets in the 1800s evolve into vehicles for hire on the street, known popularly as 'cabs'. By 1903, small numbers of petrol-powered cabs are plying for hire on the streets of London. Taxi meters displaying the fixed fares – disliked by cab drivers at first because they prefer to negotiate their own charges – are introduced the following year, and while these early London taxis are popular with the well-off in a hurry, the numbers of licensed cabs for hire remain small, just 11,862 by 1913. Horse-drawn cabs continue to ply for hire until the 1930s.

TITANIC

The *Titanic*, then the world's largest passenger steamship, struck an iceberg and sank four days out during its maiden voyage from Southampton to New York in April 1912. Over 1,500 of the estimated 2,224 passengers perished. Those who perished were mostly male – and passengers in second and third class. (The ship had far too few lifeboats on board.) Of the first-class passengers 63 per cent survived. But only 38 per cent of the third-class passengers were saved (24 per cent of the crew survived too).

Such was the class distinction of the time, the first official passenger lists released after the disaster did not even include the names of maids and servants travelling with first-class passengers. They were described as extensions of the family, simply 'Mrs J.W.M. Cardoza and Maid'. After the disaster, a rumour went around that four maids had died trapped below deck because they had been sent down to the purser's office to collect their bosses' valuables. Fortunately, it was later discovered that these four women survived. And the records show that all female servants travelling in first and second class survived. One female cook in second class survived, but one female servant travelling in third class died, as did three male chauffeurs travelling in second class.

GOODBYE BATHING MACHINE

The seaside bathing machine, a roofed wooden cart similar to a garden shed but with wheels on one end, was a typically Victorian invention, segregating the sexes and preserving their modesty, even if they fancied a cooling dip on a hot day. (The Victorians claimed that bathing suits were not 'proper' clothing, to be viewed on a beach.) Men or women could only use these machines on designated separate areas of the sands. The wannabe swimmer entered the windowless machine from the back, changed, in the dark, into their somewhat restrictive bathing gear – women into a corseted bathing dress, with knickerbockers underneath their bathing skirt, though men's bathing outfits, tight all-in-one garments that reveal all when wet, were somewhat more comfortable – and the machine was then rolled into the sea. This was achieved sometimes with a horse, sometimes by a strong man, and even, at times, by means of a mechanical contraption that dragged the whole thing into the water. Once in the water, people could take a dip, immersing themselves up to the neck, so there was no chance of any part of them being exposed to the naked eye. Their swim over, a small flag on the machine was raised – to indicate to an attendant that they wished to return to shore.

Fortunately, by Edwardian times, mixed bathing has started to become more socially acceptable and technically, legal segregation of bathing ends in 1901, though some seaside resorts are more forward thinking than others. Bexhill's move to mixed bathing causes raised eyebrows initially. But in time, the bathing machines stay on the beach as changing rooms until they disappear in 1914.

TAKING TO THE SKIES

Flying is strictly for the rich elite. In 1903, the US aviation pioneers, the Wright Brothers, make the world's first-ever powered flight. Yet commercial air travel does not start in the UK until 1919 with the first passenger service between London and Paris – which eventually goes out of business. By 1925, just over 11,000 passengers travel by air around the UK and abroad. But the numbers taking domestic or international flights don't reach the millions until the late 1950s.

Chapter 10

Morals & Manners

It's midnight in the big country house. The party guests are nearly all in their rooms. A frock-coated gentleman, loosening his cravat, is making his way down a long corridor. Thanks to the discretion of the hostess, he already knows the object of his desire is on the same floor – but where? Peering at the discreet little brass frames on each door, he checks for the name. Ah, here she is. Confidently, he turns the brass handle and steps into the spacious bedroom. A fire crackles in the big grate. Seconds later, the pair are ridding themselves of their elaborate coverings, tugging furiously at buttons, fumbling with laces and stays, throwing waistcoat, overskirt, corset, bloomers, silk stockings, shirt, trousers, up in the air, their passion over-whelming – the evidence of their fevered, hurried coupling to be scooped up from the floor, with knowing smirks, by the servants the following day.

Welcome to adultery in Edwardian high society. Both parties are titled and married. Some people in their exclusive circle know of their affair. It's been talked of for weeks now, gossiped about across the card tables or on the huge yachts of the elite as they glide through the sparkling blue waters of the Mediterranean.

Both are known for their string of different amours. Though it is now rumoured that the man's wife, having caught him in bed with a teenage footman the year before – and having openly voiced her disgust to others – is being packed off, to their Scottish estate by her parents. And, of course, downstairs chatter between the housemaids the next morning is lively and speculative. Everyone downstairs knows about the footman because his aristocratic lover promptly sacked him after being caught in the act. And the boy tried, unsuccessfully, to get a job with another posh family. The disgusted wife's lady's maid blabbed downstairs, too. But does the bisexual man's latest love know about the footman? And does she care?

She probably does know, given how discreetly bitchy the women in her circle can be. Subtle but clear hints have been dropped into her ear over tea in gilded salons. Yet she won't be questioning her lover about it. Her own marriage, since she had her son and daughter, is a sterile, hands-off relationship and she relishes the sheer thrill of the romantic, clandestine affair, the midnight assignations, partly through desire and physical need for passionate lovemaking – but also because it is so exciting to organise these stolen moments of abandon in a stiflingly boring life dominated by appearances and the rules.

Outwardly, she is a glittering hostess in the social firmament, not yet thirty, decked in jewels, silks and furs, her glamour and beauty celebrated everywhere. But her private life is a hot topic. She's aware that certain people in her circle know what's going on – yet she dare not discuss her secret love life with anyone. Only in unanswered letters to her lover does she give voice to her innermost feelings and emotions… a dangerous exercise should they fall into the wrong hands.

Yet again, the moral code of Edwardian high society dictates that the superficial is what counts. In fact, there is a long-held mantra that a respectable society woman's name only ever appears in a newspaper at birth, on marriage and on her demise. Newspapers, of course, will report the official engagements of high society. But if it all explodes into scandal and a widely reported court case – which it infrequently does – then it's open season on those who are 'caught'. And social death.

Essentially, the code permits married wealthy people to cover up their love affairs with a finely woven web of discretion and manners. If they are caught out by their spouse, the aggrieved party cannot make a scene or a noisy fuss. That just isn't permitted. Etiquette matters so much more than a discreet affair between marrieds, though at times, of course, very human emotional responses break through the web of discretion.

The royal marriage of 'Bertie' and Alexandra, which lasts for nearly 50 years and produces six children, survives scandal after scandal, mostly thanks to Alexandra's tolerance, is the upper-crust benchmark: have your cake and eat it. But keep shtum.

The social code is such that only married women can have affairs: single high-born women are hands off as far as amorous cheating husbands are concerned. Women either marry – or are married off – or they remain spinsters, a lowly status in this world. Single means 'unwanted'.

If a daring, spirited unmarried aristocratic young woman does indulge herself with a lover and falls pregnant, it's usually hushed up. A lengthy trip to Europe, accompanied by a lady's maid, is usually discreetly arranged by her family. And the child is born far away from the eyes of her peer group – the baby handed to a convent. But there is no return to society: one mistake and you're out. And since wealthy aristocratic single women are not required to pursue any profession or work, their sole purpose is to be decorative and 'come out' – and be available for invitations to dances, balls or marriage proposals. They may get intellectually involved with the issues of the day and have opinions on the social changes that are emerging around them. And this generation is often intelligent and curious. But as single women their involvement with the affairs of the world must remain limited – unless they wish to wage war with their family.

Divorce, as already seen, means loss of status, an unwanted consequence. So the big country-house gathering of 'Saturday to Monday' guests tends to be a common setting for these not-so-secret affairs; couples, given the space between them, can organise these assignations in the perfect place for 'playing away' – and extra marital bliss. In fact, this situation is so widely accepted in the elite circle that in a few big houses, the lady of the house discreetly instructs staff to ring a bell at 6am – to give certain guests a chance to get back to their own rooms before the maids start arriving with the early morning tea.

The alternative setting for illicit love is the briefer *cinq à sept* assignation (literally, 5–7pm) so beloved of the French. The venue is usually the London townhouse, where the lady changes into her fashionable tea gown, a floaty, loose, flimsy gown worn without a corset underneath, before greeting her lover. The tea dress has been created as a leisure dress (a sort of equivalent to a Juicy Couture tracksuit, though somewhat more feminine), a light, un-corseted garment that is perfect for love: a welcome improvement on the button-tugging, corset-removing marathon involved when relinquishing formal evening gear.

Such afternoon diversions are often arranged by a series of notes delivered to and from respective town houses, proffered on silver dishes by the servants – or even via the odd telegram. Phone calls, if the family use one, are too tricky. The phone is frequently kept in a hallway, where everyone can hear every word. Especially the butler...

Couples may pretend not to know about their partner's dalliances, but nothing private gets past the personal servants. Take the lady's maid. She's looks after her mistress's underwear. She knows whether her mistress is having a period. Or not. The fine linen sheets too, changed by the servants, tell their own story. It's all very well having people around to do everything for you. But if you want to keep your love life secret, forget it. When it comes to the amours of their bosses, the servants' hall is an early twentieth-century version of Twitter.

Yet if they want to keep their jobs – and sometimes a straight face – they must pretend not to see or hear anything. 'Do not seem in any way to notice, or enter into, the family conversation, or the talk at the table, or with visitors..' warns the toffs' servants' etiquette manual, *Rules for the Manners of Servants in Good Families* in 1901. So, should they unexpectedly enter a room to find a half-clad couple entwined behind a sofa, they must remain impassive, stony-faced. Only when they're downstairs can they give way to laughter and ribaldry.

In a world where TV and radio have not yet emerged, their boss's secrets are an ongoing form of gossipy entertainment for servants: the most simple task, like emptying a wastepaper basket in the living area and discovering a torn-up love letter, carelessly thrown away but pieced together by the finder, gives plenty of talk below stairs – and reveals innermost truths about their masters' emotional lives.

But what happens if one of these covert relationships results in pregnancy, you wonder? Scandal and rejection by society? Not always. Some high-born marriages just carry on regardless. One of the Edwardian era's most beautiful young aristocrats, Lady Diana Manners, is the youngest daughter of the 8th Duke of Rutland and his wife Violet. But society gossips swear that she is the illegitimate offspring of the writer, MP and womanising politician Henry Cust.

Whatever the gossips say, this does not faze Lady Diana, whose parents, at one point, pin their hopes on her marrying Edward VII's second son George (who becomes George V after the death of his father in 1910; Edward and Alexandra's first born, Albert, died of pneumonia in 1892). Eventually, Lady Diana marries another aristocrat, Duff Cooper in 1919. Celebrated as the most beautiful woman in England, such is the passion that Lady Diana inspires that her husband-to-be writes to her during their courtship: 'I hope everyone you like better than me will die very soon.'

Yet servants' unique access to upstairs' private lives can lead to temptation, too. In 1911, *The Times* newspaper reports a potential trade between an English servant and an American newspaper. An English butler, advertising for a new position, is approached by an American female journalist. She offers him monthly sums of money in exchange for gossip and tittle-tattle about leading British socialites: American readers are eager to read stories about the English aristocracy, especially anything remotely scandalous about their financial or marital woes. The butler and *The Times*' readers are shocked. But a seed is sown for less loyal servants hoping to make a quick buck. Cold cash for celebrity scandal: sounds familiar, doesn't it?

However this moral code where adultery is discreetly condoned is just one side of the dualistic nature of toff morality. Because many of these aristocratic women, whether they play around or not, have their other obligations: their involvement with charities and helping the less fortunate. And it is the same society ladies who sit on the committees that run the charities, oversee the fund-raising local bazaars, dinners and balls, the church sales, helping raise the money to fund cottage hospitals, that may be indulging in this extra-marital, secret, but not secret, world.

Charity work is part of the rules that surround their lives, of course, but a different side of the coin: helping the needy at a time when the State has yet to take responsibility for the less fortunate. Many middle-class women too are heavily involved, of course. Yet the big country house, with all its political social networking, is still at the heart of much charity, alongside the frivolity and double standards of the times. Some country-house wives are involved with organisations like the anti-alcohol movement, the Temperance Society, since alcohol is very much viewed as a social evil, especially among the poor. And, of course, it is sometimes the wife who encourages her husband to make much-needed improvements to the homes on the estate, to ease the living conditions of their tenants. Over 1,000 different charities are being run in the UK in the early 1900s, mostly headed by wealthy or middle-class women – and over half of these charities exist to help women in need.

THE UNMARRIED DAUGHTER

But what of the aristocratic daughter? If she has brothers, their path in life is set in stone: Harrow, Eton, an inherited seat in the House of Lords and eventually the cares of the family estate. But as an unmarried young woman, she can have neither affairs nor a career. Educated at home by a governess, fluent in French and German, she plays the piano beautifully and is an excellent horsewoman. But essentially, all her 'training' is for marriage, her presentation at Court during her first Season, her introduction to the rules of society.

In the meantime, there are all the customs and manners of polite society to take her into adulthood: even if she does become engaged, she is not expected to travel unaccompanied with her fiancé, for example – and such is the morality of the times, once she is 'out' in society, there are many lines she cannot cross if she wishes to be accepted by her peers. Even her hairdo plays a part. A lady may only be seen in public with upswept hair. Loose hair is regarded as a symbol of immorality, or promiscuity: a lady only permits herself to be seen this way by her spouse. Or her lady's maid.

And there are other small but important social niceties that must be followed, now that the world is changing. Young women, just like the Earl of Grantham's daughters in *Downton Abbey*, are becoming preoccupied with 'new' ideas and social etiquette, which their elders would never have permitted. Etiquette itself changes to adapt to the new ways…

- **Smoking:** Previously a male habit, smoking is gradually becoming socially acceptable for women – though some still find it deplorable. The new etiquette says that a lady should take her present company's inclination into consideration before indulging.
- **Motoring:** In the motorcar, ladies must carry hairpins and a hand mirror. These are seen as indispensible aids to attractive travelling.
- **Make-up:** Advice for those considering painting their face states that there is a right way and a wrong way of doing it. The art of concealing is very important. Anyone powdering and painting in imitation of singers and actresses must remember that these women are usually seen at a distance.

MANNERS FOR VISITORS

Because the toffs are so determined to keep their world intact and keep everyone beneath them at a distance, there is a very strict code of manners to be followed when it comes to paying calls on each other: all must follow the etiquette of the calling card.

Essentially, this system enables the upper crust to maintain formal relationships with those in the same group – and keeps out the unwanted or the social pariahs who fall from grace.

The traditional etiquette of early twentieth-century card-calling in London makes emailing seem positively blissful. A lady cannot call on another person without first presenting her calling card, via a servant. And so she may go out and about in her carriage, passing a footman her calling card to be presented at a certain grand address. (Sometimes she might keep the appropriate distance between them by telling him the address via a speaking tube.) On reaching the address, the footman rings the doorbell and the door is opened by a butler or maid. The card is then handed over with the compliments of the lady, the footman enquiring if the other lady is 'at home' today. The front door is then closed. Inside the house, staff check whether their boss is 'at home'. If she is, the footman then helps his lady out of the carriage, into the house – and must remain standing outside until the visit is over. (If she's out, the card is then kept on a silver tray in the hallway so it can be seen when she returns.)

At times, this process is accelerated by the footman being dispatched to travel around the city alone, taking calling cards from house to house, in order to demonstrate that their boss is in town.

Even the calling cards themselves follow strict etiquette. They must be plain with the gentleman's name smaller than the lady's, with the name and address printed in an ordinary typeface. Married couples have their names together on one card. Unmarried daughters have their names placed beneath their mother's.

And typically, once an introduction has been made through a mutual friend, a formal call must be returned within three to four days. After a dinner or a ball, it is necessary for a guest to call or leave their card at the host's house within the next few days. Calling hours are strictly between 3–6pm. To call before luncheon is socially unacceptable. ('A call' is not the same as 'a visit'; a visit means spending at least one night away from home.)

Once these rituals have been observed, there are other rules to observe:

- The first call should be short, about 15 minutes. Conversationally, topics may only be light and superficial. No talk of politics, religion or anything remotely controversial. Nor should dogs or children accompany the visitor.

- For the afternoon call, a coat or cloak may be taken off. But a lady must keep her hat on (this is probably more to do with the fact that the hats are so enormous and hairdos are so elaborate, it requires careful help from a lady's maid to take it on and off). A gentleman is permitted to bring his hat and stick into the room and keep it in his hands or on the floor. Only after this first call – and provided it has gone well – can a dinner invitation be issued.

- When country house families travel to London for the Season, their cards are marked PPC (*Pour Prendre Congé*, translated from French and meaning 'to say goodbye'). And when they are back in their country estate, the same rituals must be observed when making social calls in the area. A few aristocrats ignore all this, mainly because they are so grand, they don't need to bother, yet even by 1911, the etiquette manual, *Etiquette of Good Society*, written by Lady Colin Campbell, tells calling card dissenters: 'Visits of form of which most people complain and yet to which most people submit, are absolutely necessary – being in fact the basis on which that great structure, society, mainly rests. You cannot invite people into your house, however often you may have met them elsewhere, until you have first called upon them in a formal manner and they have returned the visit. It is a kind of safeguard against any acquaintances which are thought to be undesirable.'

SECRET VICES

'Undesirable acquaintances' in their social clique may be avoided by a strict code of manners, yet the morals of the upper crust remain silently tolerant of other sexual habits.

Given the prevailing Christian ethos of the times, prostitution is still very much frowned upon. In the Victorian years, religious reformers, backed by the Church of England, sponsor many groups to help 'fallen women' into situations where they might be reformed, but these are mostly unsuccessful: at the start of the Edwardian era in London alone an estimated 80,000 prostitutes are walking the streets.

Various attempts to close down brothels also fail. And in one notorious episode in 1889, the Cleveland Street scandal, a homosexual male brothel offering rent boys for hire is discovered by police – and the investigation reveals that one of its key clients is Lord Arthur Somerset, an equerry to the Prince of Wales and son of the 8th Duke of Beaufort. (Lord Arthur is never charged and spends the rest of his life abroad.)

Yet the 'invisible' but very real trade of sex for cash or a visit to a brothel remains a huge draw for the privileged and moneyed classes. It's the place where younger men pay to learn about love – and older men get their particular tastes or whims serviced. Wives often understand this, and look away. Discretion is more or less assured when travelling, so the more popular brothels with the English toffs tend to be in Paris, the city of love. A big favourite with the Prince of Wales – in his party years before he takes the throne – is Le Chabanais, a luxurious, lavishly decorated house of pleasure near the Louvre where the Prince's own room (decorated with his own coat of arms) includes a copper bathtub, decorated with a half-swan, half-woman figure, where he reputedly soaks in champagne with one or two girls. The room also has an interesting chair, called a *siege d'amour* (a love seat). Here, the Prince cavorts to his heart's content with his favourite party girls. Yet again, those in his elite circle take their lead from 'Bertie' – and continue, through the Edwardian years, to pursue their own pleasures with those of the world's oldest profession.

MORALS AND THE DOWNSTAIRS STAFF

The servants, of course, don't have the luxury of the hypocritical double-standard morality of their masters. After all, they're on the premises, all the time, to pick up the evidence of their employers' bed-hopping – and they may even wind up helping to bring up the illegitimate offspring of their bosses, passed off as one of the family. So some cynicism, particularly among the uppers, is understandable.

But it's the younger female servants who have the most to lose if they don't follow all the rules, given the sexual segregation of the house – and the concerns around 'followers' and pregnancy, though some bosses profess not to want servants to get pregnant out of pure self interest but out of deep concern for their moral welfare. They dress it up that way, of course, especially in a country house with its own chapel and prayers twice a day. But the truth is, some people upstairs just don't want their servants to have any life of their own – it might get in the way of having them at their beck and call.

As for the girls entering service at 13 or 14, they are often innocent. For some, the Bible may be the only book they've ever read; their religious beliefs are quite strong. Yet despite much debate in the early twentieth century about introducing sex education to address ignorance, it remains very much an unresolved issue. Nor is there any contraception – and sexually transmitted diseases are a real problem (see Chapter 12). So the girls, largely ignorant of such things, work for employers who are usually happy to keep them in ignorance. A pregnant servant is an unwanted commodity. And it would not be unknown for an observant housekeeper, concerned about one-too-many pairs of male eyes lingering over a pretty young housemaid, to demand to check the housemaid's washable sanitary wear, just to make sure she's not pregnant. If she is, she's more likely to want to keep it secret as long as possible – or try to do something about it herself.

It may be difficult now to understand such behaviour, but a hundred years ago, young people of all classes did not really have the opportunity to indulge in pre-marital sex to the same degree as nowadays. For a start, young people, including those not working in service, were much less free to go their own way: folk lived in small areas or neighbourhoods where everyone knew everyone else's business.

Locally, small towns and city areas had the 'monkey walk', which was effectively a pre-courtship ritual among 14–15 year olds. The youngsters would congregate in a specific part of town and the boys would hang around just watching the girls go past. But that was it. Everything in society, social pressure, beady-eyed employers and lack of education conspires against the unlucky single young woman who finds herself with a dependent child, no husband and little – or no – money. The social stigma that goes with having an illegitimate baby is very strong, the entire responsibility placed with the female; even if the young girl has been raped and falls pregnant, there is little to help her – unless she can find someone to marry her. If not, the best she might hope for is a roof over her head with her family, if they accept her back with a baby. Then, if she's lucky, she might be able to take in sewing or washing if she's picked up those skills. It pays a pittance, but it's what millions of women do at home in order to survive – even if they don't have illegitimate children.

Are the servants immoral? Not really. There are always some who might be tempted to steal from their employers – but it's more likely to be through necessity or foolishness than sheer greed. And if there's a question mark over the morality of the upper servants who take a 'cut' from the tradespeople they deal with all the time, the butlers and housekeepers taking advantage of a discount which they then pocket, this is more of a perk of the job than a lapse in moral standards. Considering the immense wealth around them and the years they've already spent in service earning low wages, it would be strange if they didn't take advantage of these perks.

So while there's a certain amount of hanky panky going on upstairs between consenting adults, the morals of the country-house inhabitants, while not exactly squeaky clean, probably aren't that different to what you'd find in many places nowadays, given the constraints of their society, where men are more or less permitted their sexual freedoms and women remain trapped by class and convention. And it must be remembered, too, that not all country houses are run by despots. They might be run by a very Christian, churchgoing morality – some housekeepers even ask if prospective servants are Church of England at interview stage, and servant-seeking households placing advertisements might even stipulate their religious preference – but it is the human element of this world, not the façade, that determines what it is. There are people in this house, upstairs and down, that are loyal, thoughtful, kind, decent, hardworking and sometimes religious, including some who own these estates. And there are others, including the servants, who will lie or cheat and connive their way through life, though most, rich or poor, have no option but to keep their innermost thoughts to themselves. So both ends of society are hemmed in by impossibly rigid rules. That's the one thing they do have in common.

THE KING'S LOOSE BOX

When Edward VII takes the throne in 1902, a special pew is set aside in Westminster Abbey for the sole use of his current and former lovers, the actress Lillie Langtry, Alice Keppel (Camilla Parker Bowles, the Princess of Wales's great grandmother), Daisy Greville, Countess of Warwick, Jennie Jerome (Winston Churchill's mother), 'Patsy' Cornwallis-West and Georgiana, Countess of Dudley.

Lillie, the first widely acknowledged royal mistress, has been the royal mistress for nine years. A humble clergyman's daughter with red-gold hair and a flawless complexion, at one stage she appeared in advertisements for Pears soap – one of the first twentieth-century celebrities to do so. Showered with jewels and luxury by Bertie, he is reputed to have complained: 'I spend enough on you to buy a battleship.' Lillie's retort was: 'And you spend enough in me to float one.'

WILD ABOUT HARRY

Over time, the truth about Harry Cust's many relationships with aristocratic women comes to light. Lady Diana Cooper's real father is Harry Cust, and there are other illegitimate aristocratic children sired by the priapic Harry.

'So much of the Cust strain entered England's peerage, and that from such a number of cradles, there gazed babies with eyes like large sapphires instead of the black boot buttons of their legal fathers,' says author Anita Leslie in her book, *The Marlborough House Set*. Yet Harry's many love affairs are not always quietly condoned by his lovers' husbands. Theresa, Lady Londonderry, wife of the 6th

Marquess of Londonderry, has her love letters to Harry discovered by a rival for his affections, Gladys, Lady Ripon. (Theresa's motto: 'I am a Pirate. All is fair in love and war'.) The furious Gladys wraps the letters up, ties them with a bow, and sends them directly to Theresa's husband, Charles. After reading them he leaves them in his wife's boudoir with a note: 'henceforth we do not speak', and the betrayal is never forgotten. The couple are rumoured to never speak to each other again in private for thirty years. Even when Charles is dying and his wife writes him a note asking for a deathbed reunion, he refuses to see her.

WHEN SERVANTS TELL...

The divorce trial of Lady Colin Campbell and Lord Colin Campbell, MP and youngest son of the 8th Duke of Argyll in 1886 is one of the longest divorce trials in the history of the Victorian years – and among its biggest scandals. Married for six years, both parties accuse each other of adultery. Lord Colin claims that his wife has had four lovers: a duke, a general, a doctor and a fire chief. And much to Lady Campbell's horror, a number of her senior servants appear in court as witnesses for her husband. Their 'behind the scenes' reports provide devastating evidence against their former mistress. Although both parties are shunned by polite society after the divorce is granted to her husband, Lady Colin – real name Gertrude Blood – eventually makes a new life for herself as a journalist. One of her favourite topics? Er... etiquette (she is the author of *Etiquette of Good Society*, as quoted earlier in this chapter).

ONE FINGER AND YOU'RE OUT...

Spencer Cavendish, the 8th Duke of Devonshire, and Marquess of Hartington (known as Harty Tarty) is a politician and sportsman with a somewhat rackety love life. As a young man, he is madly in love with a beautiful prostitute, Catherine Walters, known as Skittles. His parents, Lord and Lady Cavendish, do all they can to stop the affair, including packing Harty Tarty off to America for a while. On his return, they present Skittles with a Mayfair house, carriages, servants and £2,000 a year to stay away from their son. After their break-up, Skittles becomes a political hostess, entertaining the likes of Gladstone, Kitchener and the Prince of Wales.

And Harty Tarty then falls in love with the wife of the Duke of Manchester, Louisa, Duchess of Manchester; the pair conduct a 30-year affair until the Duke of Manchester dies in 1890. Two years later, Harty Tarty and Louisa marry and Louisa, now Duchess of Devonshire, becomes known as the Double Duchess and is renowned for her inimitable style of greeting people at social functions. For her inner circle of intimates, she offers three fingers of her hand. Influential guests receive two fingers in greeting. And the rest get one finger. Nonetheless, after Harty Tarty's demise in 1908, the Double Duchess continues to pay Skittles her allowance until her husband's former mistress's death twelve years later.

THE SERVANT GIRL'S WORST NIGHTMARE

Given the attitudes to illegitimacy at the time, a young servant girl who falls pregnant might attempt any number of means to get rid of the baby. A young woman may even throw herself down stairs or off a table, in the hope that she might abort. Or she might offer to move heavy furniture or do anything physically dangerous around the house. Given the sheer physicality of much of their work, such measures are part of the everyday routine of the house – though a beady-eyed colleague or housekeeper might notice and tell others in the house, including the family. Other methods include hot mustard baths or swallowing quinine tablets – or taking penny royal, an ancient herbal folk remedy, used for many ailments including flatulence and gout and reputed to bring on contractions of the uterus and help self-abort.

An early advertisement for Pears Soap.

Chapter 11

How to Wear It

Teatime. Below, the footmen are precariously balancing the artfully arranged pretty china plates of ginger biscuits, scones, egg sandwiches and chocolate cake on big silver trays as they mount the stairs to the drawing room.

Above, the lady of the house, with the help of her lady's maid, is choosing her tea gown: should it be the thick white crêpe de Chine, fringed with a netted silk and interspersed with gold and white cord tassels with a pretty lace bodice in palest gold? Or should she go for the pale grey satin and chiffon floaty gown with the delicate lace underskirt, fringed with chenille and with embroidered sleeves?

Decisions, decisions. It has to be the grey satin. Neither of these gowns have been worn before; they are the lady's very latest acquisitions from the first ever couture house, the House of Worth, founded by an Englishman, Charles Frederick Worth, in Paris, where many aristocratic wives make an annual pilgrimage to view the latest collections – and order the most exquisite, made-to-measure high-fashion garments money can buy. Every Worth gown is unique: hand-stitched luxurious fabrics with beautiful trims of pearls and jewels, priced at around £7–8,000 each in today's money.

When you are required to change outfits and accessories four to six times a day, choosing what to wear is a serious business. The task of looking good at all times involves much shopping and choosing: a month can easily slip by in leisurely, shopping-for-pleasure visits to Worth's Rue de la Paix salon as each creation is modelled (Worth is the first to use mannequins, rather than shop 'dummies' and the first ever designer to have his name sewn into the garments), mulled over, discussed at length, then fitted perfectly to the lady's form; then it is cut, hand sewn and packed in yards of tissue paper into the enormous trunks which are regularly shipped back home. It's fashionable to order half a dozen garments from each season's collection.

Those who wish to shop in London, flock to the showrooms of Maison Lucile, the elegant fashion house run by the aristocratic Lady Duff Gordon. Or they can spend time shopping in stores like Harrods or the country's first purpose-built department store, Selfridges.

Four seasons, four different collections. Day dresses for the morning; tailored day dresses for smart daytime events or even weddings; fragile ankle-length evening dresses in chiffon, satin, silk or velvet, cunningly cut to show off a slender shape; floor-length evening dresses with trains for entertaining; two-piece fine wool costumes with long narrow skirts and embroidered hems for walking, matched with long, narrow straight-cut coats, outlined with braid; brocade embroidered waistcoats; lacy handmade blouses with pretty inserts – accompanied, according to season, by long fur stoles, ostrich or marabou boas and stoles, fur-trimmed muffs and mantles: these women make the average WAG look dowdy. And, of course, there's also the jewellery, the diamonds and the pearls, the most valuable items locked away below stairs in the butler's safe; 'everyday' jewels are kept in a box on the lady's dressing table.

The wealthy Edwardian woman may not be quite as high spending as the super- rich American lady, whose passion for exquisite Paris fashion from couturiers like Worth, Paquin and Doucet exceeds anything ever known before, with hundreds of outfits and gowns being ordered in just one session.

Yet given how important her appearance is, the English aristocratic lady's boudoir has very well-stocked wardrobes, one for daywear, one for evening wear, as well as a huge armoire with big drawers beneath which holds pile upon pile of neatly folded garments. As fashion changes – and the major changes in high fashion don't start until the end of the first decade of the twentieth century – rich women's clothes, so showy and sweeping, richly adorned with frills, lace, jewels and beads, become leaner and more pared down, but they remain highly decorative. And there are major influences creeping into high fashion: beautiful leading actresses are now dressed extravagantly by the leading couturiers. Their looks attract huge public interest in newspapers and magazines when they appear at fashionable first nights. Everything about them is admired and copied, their clothes, their hair, even their mannerisms. Society women are still fêted for their style. But these actresses, with their high visibility, are cultivated by everyone, including royalty.

Every item in the mistress's wardrobe, each delicate, exquisite creation, must be beautifully looked after by her lady's maid. There's no mad dash round the corner to the dry cleaners or a last-minute chuck into the washing machine; everything is painstakingly hand-washed, with Fuller's Earth the popular method for removing greasy stains. Total responsibility for the care and repair of all these pricey designer items is all down to the lady's maid: some of the creations are made from such delicate silks, adorned with heavy jet or cut-steel bead trims which weigh down the fabric, that she must fold each one very carefully before storing it in the enormous wardrobe; hanging might tear the fabric. And her sewing machine in her room downstairs is frequently in use for repairs or alterations to the lady's wardrobe; it's one of the most valuable tools of her trade.

A country-house lady's night attire is ultra feminine: long silk hand-embroidered chemises, pumps (slippers) made of cotton sateen, handmade dressing gowns in silk or fine wool, silk or cotton camisoles, cotton pantaloons (worn as knickers), elegant bed jackets in light quilted silk or silk chiffon. Stockings are very fine silk. Handmade underwear is made from the finest Lyon silks or satins (from the nineteenth century onwards, nuns in European convents make huge amounts of lingerie for society's wealthiest women).

Her daytime footwear is often narrowly cut soft kid or patent leather-buttoned boots – narrow feet are believed to be a sign of good breeding – so all women's shoes, whatever the width of their feet, are both narrow and tight. In the evening, she wears court shoes with a small Louis heel. These are usually quite elaborate, embellished with embroidery, lace or jet beading at the toe. (There are no shoes made with synthetic materials at this time, so even the narrowest cut shoes eventually stretch and mould to the wearer's feet, sometimes stretching beyond the sole.)

It's likely that the older aristocratic grande dame (think of the Dowager Duchess of Crawley, played by Maggie Smith in *Downton Abbey*) would be unwilling to adapt to the latest innovations in high fashion: she's not as keen as her granddaughters are to indulge in the newer, more pared down look or the new hobble skirt: she prefers to stick to the gathered shoulders and huge bustles of her era – and she's less likely to discard her unwanted garments readily by handing them over to the lady's maid as the younger women do. She finds the wealthiest American women of fashion, in particular, extremely ill bred and vulgar – their rule of never ever wearing the same garment twice in public is, she insists, indicative of their lack of breeding. (They, in turn, are puzzled by the British aristocratic love of the ancient, the worn or the faded christening dress, handed down, generation after generation.) So there is still a measure of restraint in the expenditure on clothes. But not much.

HATS

Everyone in Edwardian society wears a hat. Even young girls cannot go out bareheaded. Huge hatboxes accompany the trunkfuls of clothes the society woman takes with her on her travels or for a 'Saturday to Monday'. Society women's hats are big. And they're not just ordinary hats – they are elaborate, highly decorative confections perched atop hair piled high, worn with matching gloves, shoes and stockings, sometimes with accompanying parasols of ruched chiffon or lace, complete with ivory handles.

These supremely elegant hats are often adorned or trimmed with everything you can think of: huge feathers, plumes, lace, braid, rich satin ribbons, even baskets of fake flowers; at times a long chiffon scarf, knotted underneath the chin, is deployed, to keep it all in place. The hatpins society women use to secure their hats are big steel weapons with jet, pearl or enamel ends showing through.

Hats are kept on at lunch. Sometimes, they are even worn with evening dress in restaurants and the theatre. (The famous actress of the times, Sarah Bernhardt, bans hats when she manages to finance her own theatre because the hats obstruct the audience's view of the stage.) Why are they left on so frequently? Mainly because they involve a great deal of work by the lady's maid to secure it in the first place. Alternatively, for evening wear, the upswept hairdos may be adorned with ostrich or peacock feathers and, at very grand events, tiaras or jewel-studded combs are on display.

LET ME BREATHE...

All this adornment is costly, time consuming and extravagant. And until around 1908 wearing it is sheer torture to move around in. The 'S' shaped corset, introduced in 1900 as a 'Health Corset' and adopted by all fashionable women, is supposed to follow the natural lines of the body, but in fact it forces the bosom out revealingly, nips the waist in tightly and pushes out the bottom.

This corset is hell to wear. Women are accustomed to uncomfortable corsetry, being laced in underneath, but this is extreme: the overall effect makes a woman look like her top half is way ahead of the rest of her. Given the many clothes that go underneath, the chemise, corset cover, drawers, flannel petticoat, cotton lace-trimmed petticoat and, sometimes, a silk petticoat on top of all this, it is a nightmare of restriction – and pain.

The hats too are torture, perched as they are on top of drawn-up hair, supported by pins and combs, which has been puffed out and built up over pads (known as 'rats') which are inserted along the front of the head. The elaborate hatpins spear the hat to the hair underneath. (This look works best on dirty hair; clean hair is too soft to hold all the pins.) And sometimes the sharp points of the pins are quite dangerous; there's a risk of spearing anyone who comes too close. And, of course, the hats are costly – the equivalent of three thousand pounds in today's money for one hat.

For years, there have been attempts to encourage less-restrictive clothing for women. But the real turning point in fashion comes in 1908 when Paris designer Paul Poiret banishes the curvy and distorting 'S' shape corset and brings in a more natural, straighter-line corsetry that follows the real shape of a woman's figure. The new-style corset is lower in the bust (bringing in a need for an early version of a brassiere) and thicker at the waist. It's still not comfortable by our standards – at first the new corset is too long, making sitting down a problem – but the die has been cast and women are able to stand and sit more naturally.

Gradually, bit by bit, clothes become less restrictive: the frilled Edwardian petticoats go out of fashion. And as women adopt the more comfortable 'tailor mades', the loose-waisted jackets and straight, ankle-length skirts that are easier to walk in, often worn with fox furs and big hats, high fashion starts to become more comfortable. The flimsy tea gowns become looser and plunging necklines are more common, despite lectures from the pulpit on the moral dangers of revealing more flesh.

Generally, as public attention is drawn to women's rights via the suffragettes and their quest for votes for women, women's clothes are getting more practical. By 1913 hats are flatter – but they're still big. Handbags too are starting to become more practical, large flat bags become fashionable. And outside the country-house world, this need for more practical clothing is being driven by new working women in the cities, doing jobs that were previously all-male preserves like clerks and secretaries, and wearing tailored dresses with high collars. Fashion reflects society. And the country-house society, with all its refinements and boundaries, is poised, by 1914, to change for ever…

MAKE-UP

Make-up has been considered too 'fast' for society women until now. But encouraged by the acclaimed beauty of the theatre actresses who do wear make-up and, in many ways, overtake the wealthy elite to become the leaders of fashion, some women are starting to go a bit beyond their traditional touch of powder (usually Fuller's Earth, see panel below) and a dab of lip salve, though lavender or rose water remain favourite scents.

Some more daring women are creating a white skin, by using liquid creams and rice powder (tanned skin is a traditional mark of poverty) or they might even go so far as to emphasise the violet veins around their cleavage with a blue-coloured crayon. Eyebrows too may be darkened with the help of the lady's maid, who deploys a cork singed in a lit candle. And for evenings, the lady's dancing slippers are concealed in a fashionable little drawstring Dorothy bag, made from velvet or satin and lined in silk.

Menswear

But what about the country-house man? He too must bow to the dictates of fashion and style. Evening wear, daywear, clothes to shoot in, clothes for leisure, his valet will lay out fresh outfits and help him change his attire at least three times a day. He's less restricted than his wife: the toff's tailored 'look' has been long and lean for some time. His hair is cut short by his valet and, if he has a beard, it's a bit less pointy. Moustaches are sometimes curled. His shoes are mostly boots, sometimes two-tone over-the-ankle boots with the upper half in a lighter colour than the sole, or lace-up boots in dark colours. For business, he wears Oxfords with high arches, a style still seen nowadays. Formal boots usually have white uppers, spats style, and buttons on the side. Or he might go for pumps, a cross between an Oxford and a modern woman's low-heeled shoe.

Daywear is usually a three-piece suit consisting of a lounge coat (replacing the previous fashion for a frock coat) with a matching waistcoat and sometimes with contrasting trousers. If he chooses, the jacket and trousers match and a contrasting single-breasted waistcoat is worn.

If he's bang up-to-the minute, his trousers are a bit shorter than they were before, sometimes with turn-ups. And they are sharply creased front and back. If he wants formal wear in the daytime, his valet will usually lay out a cutaway morning coat to be worn with striped trousers. And his shirt collars are very tall and stiffened.

For shooting parties, he's still shod in sturdy boots or shoes with leather gaiters, worn with the traditional country gentleman's attire, the sturdy tweed Norfolk jacket, with box pleats over the chest and at the back, complete with matching breeches, knee-length stockings and a flat cap. If he's golfing or cycling, the valet might lay out this kind of Norfolk tweed outfit, too. For sailing trips, his trunk will carry a number of navy-blue blazers or striped flannel coats cut like a sack coat with patch pockets and brass buttons. If he's really feeling informal, he might wear a striped shirt. Or a panama hat.

For dinner, at home or at his men's club, he sports a tuxedo with a shawl collar with silk or satin facings. And for really formal events, a dark tailcoat and trousers with a light or dark waistcoat is usually his chosen attire. Worn with a white bow-tie and a stiff-fronted shirt with a winged collar, or a very thin bow-tie, plus a fresh flower on his lapel, a carnation or a gardenia brought to him from the estate gardens on a silver tray.

Both men and women always wear gloves, the men's gloves usually in white, grey or tan, sometimes matching the tie or neckwear. And in winter, the entire outfit is usually topped off by a calf-length woollen overcoat. And, of course, for all formal occasions he wears a top hat, another toff status symbol he has yet to relinquish. He may not 'give a fig' for fashion itself. But he's acutely aware that his appearance, and his adherence to the dress codes of his class must send out all the 'right' messages to the world. So when he notices, while relaxing with a cigar in his club, that one or two of his cronies are using a very pleasant-smelling perfumed cologne, he recalls his valet mentioning to him that Mr Penhaligon's Hammam Bouquet is all the rage now, sir. And quite soon, he's wearing it himself.

WHAT THE SERVANTS WEAR

By complete contrast, life spent working in a grand country house means wearing uniform for most of the time. This ranges from the elegant, formal attire of the male uppers like the butler, valet or footmen, to the dark, drab uniform dresses with aprons worn by most of the female servants.

A work uniform, by tradition, is not provided for female servants, who must buy or make it themselves. Male servants wearing livery, such as footmen, have traditionally had their clothing provided for them. So the young girl entering live-in service, nervously arriving at the grand house for her first day with her clothing in a black tin trunk, may have already been obliged to borrow money to buy or make her required uniform. Sometimes she might have already been working in order to save up to go into service, perhaps by looking after children in the daytime to earn enough to find the cash for her work clothing.

Looking clean, neat and tidy yet inconspicuous is an important aspect of the rules around live-in service. So dress restrictions are usually discussed at the job interview with the housekeeper. A new housemaid will be told exactly what she needs: usually it's four dresses, two printed working cotton 'washing frocks' in dark grey or navy (these are worn with pinafores and get filthy during the morning cleaning or kitchen sessions), accompanied by a black dress, plus white cap and apron for afternoon attire. (Wearing a waist apron, rather than the lowly pinafore, denotes a slightly higher status.) The second black dress is also worn outdoors and for Sunday church. In some households, specific colour coding is worn by servants, i.e. white and grey only for nursery maids.

Headgear is a very important part of overall appearance. The rules are such that a cap must be worn at all times. In some big houses, it's not unknown for a maid caught without her cap to be sacked by the mistress, a somewhat ancient tradition which lingers on – at one stage no respectable woman could be seen outside the bedroom without covering her hair in some way. Female servants must also wear a hat or bonnet at all times when outdoors, usually a black bonnet in a hood-like shape for Sunday church visits. Expenditure for other items like boots, black stockings and underwear is also down to the employee. (Lisle stockings – lisle is a cotton fabric with a smooth finish – cost 4 pence a pair and are frequently darned time and again.)

The total cost of a new female servant's working uniform can frequently add up to as much as £3 or £4, representing several months' wages for a scullery maid. So if a new maid cannot manage to borrow from friends or family to gradually repay from her wages, the housekeeper may agree, via the mistress, that they fork out for her uniform – and deduct the cost from her pay. Hair, too, must be neat and unobtrusive: a 15-year-old housemaid with her hair severely drawn back, braided and neatly pinned usually looks much older than her years.

Of the female upper servants, the housekeeper usually wears dark, somewhat sombre and severe plain dresses, usually black with a white frill at the collar and a white lace cap. Governesses wear similar attire. Only the lady's maid is permitted to be remotely fashionably dressed, given the need for her to be up-to-date to advise her boss on the latest trends and looks. Yet she too, at interview stage, might be subjected to certain restrictions in her appearance by the housekeeper. She could be asked to remove the hidden 'rats' or pads from beneath her swept-up hairdo. Or she might be told to cut the tail off a fashionable long dress. She has to look appropriate for the lady – and the household – she works for.

In many cases, the lady's maid does not have much money to spend if she's saving up for her time off and visits to her family. So she frequently wears cast-offs, excellent quality clothes given to her by her employer (or previous employers), which she can, with the help of the sewing machine, alter to suit her shape. And, of course, while she must look good to reflect her boss's status, she can only look modestly fashionable and well turned out. Nothing too extravagant.

Tightly laced corsets are worn by all women. For a young servant this can be even more uncomfortable and constricting than the corset worn by her mistress: wealthy women's corsets have whalebone stays (supports) which are more pliant – yet poorer people's stays are made from cheaper metal. So the corsets, worn over a cotton vest and cotton bloomers, really dig into the girls' hips and stomach, let alone the discomfort of the tight waist lacing which can even make eating difficult. Given the amount of bending, stretching and kneeling the housemaids are doing as part of their everyday routine, it must have been tempting to give the corset a miss sometimes. Yet until the less restrictive underwear comes in towards the close of the Edwardian era, they must put up with it.

Boots are an expensive item for servants to buy: one new pair of handmade boots can cost around £2. In the nineteenth century when live-in servants are paid annually, payday means a trip to the local village to pay their annual account with the shoemaker, and on settling day the shoemaker celebrates – by providing a dish of stuffed chine (salt pork filled with herbs) for his customers.

MAISON LUCILE

From her early dressmaking beginnings making clothes for friends, Lucy Christiana Sutherland, known professionally as 'Lucile', a divorced woman with a small daughter, rises to prominence – via a society marriage to Scottish landowner and sportsman, Sir Cosmo Duff Gordon in 1900 – as the most important fashion designer in the country, designing exclusive, romantic, feminine and sensual lingerie, tea gowns and evening wear for royalty and the fashionable elite. (She is also the sister of acclaimed Edwardian novelist Elinor Glyn.)

Lucile is the first designer to give her clothes names, such as 'Do you Love me?' or 'When Passion's Thrall is O'er', and is an innovator of early 'catwalk' fashion shows in her plush, carpeted Hanover Square showroom where her gowns, exquisitely feminine creations of beaded and sequined embroidery, with lace inserts and garlands of tiny roses, are paraded by statuesque beauties before their elegant audience.

The Lucile brand is expanded to New York in 1910 and Paris in 1911. She and her husband are also survivors of the ill-fated *Titanic* voyage in 1912; afterwards, rumours persist for many years that Cosmo bribed the crewmen in their lifeboat not to return to the sinking ship to rescue others. After World War I, when fashions change, Lucile becomes a fashion columnist and pundit until her death in 1935.

THE MULTI-PURPOSE CLAY

Fuller's Earth is a highly absorbent clay, rich in minerals, used for a wide range of purposes including stain removal, as a skin cleanser, to help clear up spots or nappy rash and also as a dry shampoo. Mixed with water, Fuller's Earth powder makes a natural face pack to help remove blackheads and skin impurities. It can also give relief from insect bites when mixed with water and apple cider vinegar.

SHOPPING FOR PLEASURE

The growth of conspicuous consumption is significant in the Edwardian era. Shopping as a leisure activity, originally a Victorian innovation, now expands even further, thanks to greater transport facilities and the rise of the comfortably-off middle classes. Harrods in Knightsbridge is a huge draw for the elegant and wealthy as is Selfridges, whose opening in Oxford Street in 1909 draws five million people in its first five days.

Fashionable shopping hours are between 2pm and 4pm and these upmarket stores have their own extensive workrooms employing hundreds of women hand-sewing exclusive made-to-measure garments for wealthy women, frequently offering copies of Paris models. If she can't find time to get away, a country-house lady can also now order her clothes from a mail-order catalogue from big department stores, outfits which might consist of a ready-made skirt and material for the bodice or top, to be made up by the lady's maid. And aspirational middle-class women are also flocking to the other big, smart department stores in London, Edinburgh, Birmingham and Manchester. Many of these stores, like Fortnum & Mason (who started out as grocers in 1707) grow out of small specialist shops. Harrods starts life as a grocery store in 1849, and Thomas Burberry, originally a country draper, opens in London in

1904, creating clothes for the female motorist needing a special motoring coat to protect against dust and weather. Clothing brands like Jaeger start out as a 'scientific' idea promoting wool fibres for clothing, particularly underwear. This too evolves, as a number of retail stores selling men's and women's clothes made from fine natural fabrics start to open everywhere.

RATIONAL DRESS SOCIETY

Founded by Viscountess Harberton in 1880, to promote healthier fashions that do not restrict or deform the body, the society is against the wearing of tight corsets, high-heeled shoes, heavily weighted skirts and all garments impending free movement of the arms and legs. The organisation also believes that no woman should wear more than 7lb of underwear (back then, underwear was made of bulky gathered cotton and heavy wool flannel). By 1895, a few privileged women are starting to appear in rational dress consisting of loose divided skirts for biking and more tailored suits for daywear. But it's not until much later, after World War I, that fashions really start to become easier to wear and more comfortable for everyone.

LIVERY & POWDERED HAIR

Livery, a traditional and very distinctive colourful servants' outfit for men, has been worn by country-house footmen for centuries. And by the start of the twentieth century, some country-house families still require their footmen to wear livery at certain times during the day, while others prefer footmen to wear livery just for specific events, like balls or big receptions. So footmen in country houses where livery is worn at certain meals find themselves spending a great deal of time dressing and undressing. For example, they serve lunch in an outfit consisting of black trousers, waistcoat, white shirt, white bow-tie and knee-length boots. Yet when serving tea and dinner they change into scarlet livery consisting of a short scarlet coat, a scarlet waistcoat, purple knee breeches, white stockings, black pumps with bows and a square white bow-tie. (Staff sometimes buy ready-made bow-ties with a round collar, to save dressing time.)

In many aristocratic London town houses, large supplies of livery are kept in the house, only to be worn by footmen at big balls or entertainments, complete with top hats. And in a few big houses, footmen in livery are still required to have powdered hair, a hangover from the eighteenth century, when many senior servants of both sexes wore grey wigs. As well as providing the livery for footmen, some country-house owners provide the powder – or the money to buy it. Powdering hair is a lengthy process. Hair must be wet, then soap is rubbed in to produce a stiff lather so the lather can be combed through. Finally a powder puff is used liberally all over the head and left to dry until firm. Later, at night, the hair is washed and oiled to remove the powder.

A poster advertising the Weingarten Brothers' La Vida Corset.

Chapter 12

Health

How healthy are the people living in the country house? Food-wise, at least, both toffs and servants are much better off than the rest of the population. The daily diet consists of fresh, plentiful food, grown or produced on the estate. So valued is this home-grown produce, wealthy families often have some foodstuffs transported, by train, to their London town house during the Season. Yet overindulgence is such a feature of the toffs' world, because there is so much emphasis on meals and entertaining. Balanced against that, of course, there's the country-house outdoor lifestyle, the shooting, riding, hunting, tennis and cycling.

The servants' food may not be lavish, but it's still much better than the diet of most working-class people. Mostly, those in service walk on Sundays and time off – or use a bike, so their lifestyle isn't completely unhealthy.

There's much greater emphasis now on outdoor activity and sport. Edwardians have thrown off the stuffy, cluttered claustrophobic environment of the Victorians. The middle classes especially, are very keen on fresh air, getting out and about, playing sport and taking more exercise, especially women, now that they're beginning to be less restricted by clothing. The introduction of electric lighting in the cities makes getting around after dark less dangerous too.

Yet the reality is, health wise, the overall population, especially children, are no healthier now than they were half a century ago. Poverty is one big reason for this. For the majority, life is grim: there are large slum areas, shockingly overcrowded. But another reason for the lack of improvement in the nation's health is down to ignorance: nutrition, so crucial to development and wellbeing, is poorly understood by many.

The toffs are happy to make their annual visits to fashionable spa resorts and take some sort of 'cure' as a penance for their overindulgence. But they're not swallowing vitamin tablets and making carrot juice in the blender the rest of the time. The multi-course Edwardian diet is rich and unhealthy, with very large amounts of meat and considerable quantities of all manner of alcoholic drinks, plus many sugary or starchy treats on the table. So the posh digestive systems take a terrible caning. Yet they are mostly quite careless of the consequences of all this. After years of overindulging at the table, many have stomach or digestive illnesses like indigestion, gout or gallstones. Overindulgence in alcohol and smoking too – all those smoke-filled Gentlemen's Clubs and ordinary pubs – are not considered injurious to health by most. Alcoholic excess is taken seriously by the do-gooders and middle classes as a social problem of the less fortunate – the servants definitely can't be seen to be tipsy in the dining room – but the concern doesn't go beyond that.

Yet the aristos' close involvement with the politics of the time mean that some retain genuine concerns for the social welfare of their tenants and the poor. Part of their remit involves helping fund-raise or donate to local institutions like cottage hospitals, or sitting on the boards of larger teaching hospitals. But for the most part their own health, as far as their culinary excesses are concerned, does not come under too much scrutiny. However, dieting fads are now starting to surface, with US dieting gurus like Horace Fletcher getting considerable attention from the smarter sections of society.

Medicine is starting to improve. There are no antibiotics to treat bacterial infection yet (the first commercially produced antibiotics are not available until World War II), and vaccinations against killer illnesses like measles don't appear until the early sixties. Diphtheria and tuberculosis are still rife, accounting for many childhood deaths. (While vaccination for smallpox, cholera and typhoid fever are already available by the early 1900s, the first vaccines for diphtheria and tuberculosis don't arrive until the 1920s.) Nor have important social health-related issues like birth control or the prevalence of sexually transmitted diseases been tackled.

Yet by the close of the first decade of the twentieth century, there are significant advances. There's a much wider understanding of the importance of hygiene. Some progress has been made in treating infectious illnesses like diphtheria. X-ray machines are introduced – radiotherapy treatment for cancer is first used in 1900; and the improvements in surgical procedures since anaesthetics were introduced in 1846 are enhanced by the pioneering work of Glasgow surgeon, Joseph Lister (later Lord Lister), who discovers the use of antiseptics in surgery to prevent sepsis or poisoning of wounds, making operations safer. (Listerine mouthwash is named after him.)

After the introduction of free school meals in 1906, the following year the educational authorities start to undertake the medical inspection of all children at school. This system starts off slowly. But as it goes on, it proves to be a huge leap forward as a preventative health measure. Now doctors can check and control childhood ailments and physical defects. Higher nursing standards too, as promoted by the remarkable efforts of Florence Nightingale, start to take effect.

There are also new remedies and medicines available to buy over-the-counter from the chemist or apothecary. Aspirin, for instance, first goes on sale in 1905. Yet in rural areas, working people still tend to stick to the old remedies and potions, using spices, ointments and herbs: country doctors tend not to be up to speed on the newest developments. And the medicines on sale from the chemist are for the rich and well heeled. The majority of ordinary people can't afford them. Nor can they afford to visit a GP if they're sick. And so what actually takes place when illness or sickness strikes in the country house is a clear reminder of the vast unbreachable divide between those above and below stairs.

In most aspects of medical care, the rich use their money to enjoy better quality medical services than the poor. The sole exception to this, until the early twentieth century, is hospital care. Mostly, the poor rely on charity – or traditional remedies.

The toffs can afford the best medical help available. The presence of a leading specialist in any field can be requested should they wish. Their eminent, respected doctors mostly treat royalty and the elite. Local, respected country doctors are sometimes called upon, but the toffs have the luxury of going after the 'second opinion'. Or third. Which is not always such a good idea if the doctors disagree.

Having a retinue of servants around to help in a sickroom means hospital is not always required, even if surgery is involved, since the wealthy family can, if they wish, have a surgical procedure performed at home. But most country-house mistresses will travel to a private nursing facility in

London to give birth: country doctors are not always trusted when it comes to something as important as childbirth.

When children fall ill, too, there are always nursery staff in place to look after them. The country-house childhood of Viola Bankes and her siblings, the upper-crust family living at the vast Kingston Lacy estate in Dorset (as mentioned in Chapter 6) is a perfect example of this:

'When Daphne, Ralph and I were young, the nursery and school room suite often became a children's hospital. There was always a trained nurse in residence for Ralph [her young brother]. Irish nurse Collins followed Nurse Startin, then Jewish Nurse Levy was rushed from London when we had chicken pox, the local doctor from Wimborne lamenting that it was a 'great responsibility' looking after us. Chicken pox gave way to measles, then scarlet fever, then diphtheria and whooping cough. Ralph even managed to acquire conjunctivitis after being sneezed over by an elephant in the zoo.'

She goes on to describe the medicines on offer: 'In the nursery, the principal remedy was called 'Blue Magnesia' [magnesium oxide, used with water to relieve indigestion, heartburn and constipation] because it was kept in a bottle wrapped round with blue paper to keep out the light. It was a clear liquid of no taste or use but perhaps it occasionally healed by suggestion.

'The detested castor oil was found in every nursery cupboard then. For bruises, we had a sweet smelling ointment in a small shapely jar called 'Pomade Divine', shortened to 'ma-divine' by us. When styes, boils and abscesses lodged with us, probably because we were over-fed, we would wander down to the kitchen where little Jinky [a kitchen maid] would whisk up a frothy, yellow liquid made from Brewer's yeast.'

When little Ralph slides down the banister of the big

staircase in the Kingston Lacy house, right onto the stone floor and breaking his arm in three places, amputation is initially advised by a doctor.

'But Mama withheld her permission. Luckily, she knew a brilliant surgeon, William Arbuthnot Lane, who later became a baronet when he operated successfully on a princess of the Royal House. Sir Arbuthnot [...] was a gentle, amiable, quietly spoken man with fearless, steel grey eyes. He performed operations on fractures which other doctors treated cautiously, though often very inadequately, without surgery. He was one of the first surgeons to insist on the use of sterile caps, masks and gowns and pioneered a 'no touch' technique, using long-handled instruments.'

Following the operation, Ralph's arm heals. He subsequently learns to play the violin, becomes a good horseman and can shoot well, too.

Sir Arbuthnot's methods of close observation of the patient, and similar work by Dr Joseph Bell in Edinburgh, help inspire the creation of the famous fictional detective, Sherlock Holmes. And Sir Arbuthnot is called in again by Henrietta Bankes to successfully remove Viola's appendix when she is thirteen.

'I soon recovered and there were magnificent compensations at the time. In the London nursing home, I acquired a taste for Ovaltine [a hot chocolate malt drink, first launched in 1909], which I had never come across before and my appetite was coaxed back into life by the most delicious fish soufflés.'

Viola's recollections make it clear that a sick child in the upstairs part of the house is treated in comfort at home or in a private hospital or nursing home. The aristocratic children are unlikely to wind up in the local cottage hospital, the most common source of medical care in country areas. Initially, these small cottage hospitals are funded by patient contributions and donations. As they grow in popularity, they are mostly supported by local fund-raising events run by the rich landowners and aristocrats. They're not as good as the big teaching hospitals in the cities. And then, as now, quality of care sometimes depends on location. But some do have operating theatres where GPs or consultants can carry out operations.

WHEN SERVANTS FALL ILL…

So what happens when one of the below stairs staff falls sick? Traditionally, the aristocratic families take responsibility for their servants' healthcare, especially those growing old after a lifetime of service. Old servants who can't work any more are frequently well treated as faithful retainers: in some instances, they get a cottage or almshouse on the estate to live out their last years. Employers are not paying pensions because it is considered that country-house servants are well paid and could save.

Nonetheless, because the landed gentry and aristocrats then become actively involved in helping fund local hospitals, there is initially a system in place where free medical care is provided for rural local people via tickets handed out to the poorest families in the area. Sometimes servants benefit from this ticket system of free local medical care. Their relatives or families too might access some form of healthcare support, if there are working people in the family, by using subsidised Benefit Clubs, available to everyone in the local community.

The first port of call for any servant feeling unwell or sick is the housekeeper. Part of her remit is to keep a well-stocked medicine cabinet to dish out a variety of ointments and remedies for certain complaints and ailments. She may not have all of the following items in her cupboard, but these are some of the remedies and chemical concoctions people use at this time. Many can be purchased over-the-counter at the chemist's shop without any kind of prescription:

- Smelling salts (if someone feels faint)
- Castor oil (to help digestion and avoid constipation)
- Camphorated oil (to ease coughs and chest complaints)
- Eucalyptus oil (sometimes taken on sugar cubes to swallow, to help ease coughs and kill bacteria in sickrooms)
- An inhaler like Wright's Coal Tar Vaporizer (for blocked noses or coughs)
- Poultices made from mustard and hot water spread on a flannel (for sore throats)
- Sloan's Liniment (for rubbing onto sore muscles)
- Peppermint oil with hot water (for indigestion)
- Arrowroot powder (a herbal remedy to treat stings and alleviate nausea; also useful for food poisoning)
- Fuller's Earth ointment (for cuts or burns)
- Gregory's Powder (a vile tasting mixture of rhubarb, ginger and magnesia, used as a laxative)
- Calomel (a dangerously toxic compound of mercury and chloride, used as a laxative and diuretic)

Branded cough medicines are popular, too. Hallston's Cough Medicine is one such medicine – but the problem with medicines like these is that they sometimes contain large quantities of ether or opium and are quite addictive. Housemaids are known to become so keen on them, they secrete a bottle under their mattress: they aid sleep but also produce a not unpleasant woozy, trance-like state. So the housekeeper usually keeps such cough medicines in a separate place – the poisons cupboard is really the best place for them. Another popular medication, which the toffs usually source on their travels to France, is a small, pretty tin of tablets called Cachets Faivre, pain relief medications containing quinine and caffeine, to be taken for bad headaches or migraines.

Like the cough mixtures, some of the chemical compounds are known today to be toxic and quite dangerous to use. In the seventeenth and eighteenth centuries, country-house staff frequently concocted a wide range of herbal potions and remedies, in the times when branded medicines were not widely available and the entire estate was very much a self-sufficient enterprise. And so the older, traditional remedies continue to be quite effective.

But what's the next step if the housekeeper's medicine cabinet can't help or the illness is quite serious? This is very much down to the household, the relationship between the housekeeper and the staff – and the attitude of the family towards their servants' health. Paying for a doctor to tend a sick servant is, for some wealthy families, a step they don't want to take. Ever. Tragically, Viola Bankes's story confirms this:

'The servants received very different treatment when they were ill. Usually, their sufferings passed unnoticed, they themselves being too modest and too loyal to our mother to mention them. Just as our nursery maid, Alice, had died of neglected appendicitis, so Beatrice Christopher, a third housemaid, was, much too late, discovered to have tuberculosis.'

And therein lies the problem. Even if they are sick and in need of a doctor, the hierarchical system of the house means that some servants are unlikely to make a fuss beyond talking to the housekeeper about their ailments. Sometimes they suffer in complete silence, perhaps out of a misplaced loyalty, perhaps out of fear of being unable to work. Despite the advances in medicine, sickness and early death are still very much part of the Edwardian world: for every 1,000 babies born, 150 don't make it to the age of five.

So while the mistress of the house, accompanied by her older daughters, continues to fund-raise and make her regular visits around the estate, delivering soup, handing out unwanted clothing, dispensing to the needy, if a tenant pipes up and mentions their concerns about any kind of illness, they get sympathy, soup or kindly concern. But not necessarily a doctor. In the fictional *Downton Abbey* household of kindly Lord Grantham (Hugh Bonneville), the cook, Mrs Patmore (Lesley Nicol), needs a visit to an eye specialist – which is subsidised by her generous employer. It's a moving scenario. But in reality, it's not always the case.

THE SHOCKING TRUTH

While the country's overall standard of living improves in the early years of the twentieth century, this does not apply to a huge chunk of the working population.

First of all, house rents have gone up, thanks to rate increases, to pay for the draining and lighting improvements in the cities. As a result, the working poor fork out a large percentage of their earnings in rent, leaving them with little to spend on food, clothing and basic necessities. And they often live in horrendously overcrowded conditions, leading to the spread of illnesses like tuberculosis.

Two important social surveys of the times reveal the shocking truth:

Charles Booth, a wealthy ship owner, investigates living conditions in London in the years 1889–1907 in a series of volumes entitled *Life and Labour of the People of London*. What emerges is that almost one person in three in the capital lives in continuous poverty. And about one tenth of London's population is driven to crime to survive, many constantly living on the edge of starvation.

This follows Seebohm Rowntree's house-to-house survey of the city of York, a relatively prosperous railway town. In 1901, Rowntree's work entitled *Poverty: A Study of Town Life*, reveals that

28 per cent of the people of York earn less than the minimum amount needed to meet the basic needs of a household.

In other parts of the country, poverty is even more shocking. In 1914, around a third of everyone living in Newcastle-upon-Tyne and Sunderland lives more than two to one room, and in Scotland, nearly half the population live in houses with only one or two rooms. In mining villages in Glamorgan, Durham and Staffordshire the unpaved streets are caked with filth – and these are villages almost entirely without drains.

All this underlines the fact that country-house servants still feel, in many ways, that they are more fortunate than most. Yet one significant development between 1911 and 1912 places millions of working people at the heart of a rapidly growing new attitude to social problems. Back in the Victorian years, poverty and deprivation are accepted as part of life. Now, it is believed that the Government ought to step in to address the huge inequalities in society.

The Old Age Pensions Act for over-seventies on low incomes is introduced in 1908. And in 1911, the ruling Liberal Party politicians, and the then Chancellor of the Exchequer, David Lloyd George, want to go much further with a system of national health insurance. Germany and New Zealand have already pioneered such schemes. Now, Lloyd George's proposals for a contributory health insurance scheme, where employers, workers and the State all contribute small sums of money, by means of stamps placed on cards, will make health insurance compulsory for workers earning less than £160 a year. It means that every insured worker is entitled to medical care by a doctor, and a weekly sickness benefit (7s 6d a week for women, 10s for men) for twenty-six weeks if they are unable to work.

There is huge opposition to this. Some employers don't welcome the idea of the extra cost. The doctors' professional body, the British Medical Association, furiously denounces it. Petitions and demonstrations opposing the new scheme take place on the streets. Newspapers with big middle-class readerships come out against it. Nonetheless, the National Health Insurance Act is introduced in July 1912. It's a major reform for the lower-paid worker. It helps safeguard health and make the nation fitter. Yet many servants and their bosses are not in favour of the new scheme. Some servants resent the idea of money being taken from their meagre pay packets. But whatever their feelings, the Act marks the beginning of something much greater, the beginning of what eventually comes to be called the Welfare State to be created after 1945. And although within two years, the onset of World War I with Germany will create havoc with everyone's lives, rich or poor, the ties binding the servants to their masters are loosened: they will no longer have to rely on their masters' goodwill if they choose to seek out treatment for their ailments or illnesses.

THE COST OF MEDICAL CARE

In the nineteenth century the 'deserving poor' received free medical and surgical treatment in charitable or voluntary hospitals by means of a system where they had to produce a letter of admission written by a wealthy benefactor or employer. The very poor or old could obtain free care through Poor Law hospitals (usually infirmaries attached to workhouses), though these were transferred to the care of local authorities in 1926. Over time, the voluntary hospitals start to offer good treatment and medical facilities. So if a poor person needs an operation, they can receive top-quality free treatment in a big city teaching hospital. By the early twentieth century, these hospital facilities become sought after by everyone. Upper- and middle-class people can receive their paid-for treatment in private wards if they wish. Or they pay for treatment in a private hospital or nursing home. The fees are strictly for the rich: four guineas (£4, 4s) for a week in a private hospital in 1902.

People who can't afford private care but are not poor enough to qualify for charity must either use some form of insurance or pay a direct contribution towards the cost of hospital care. Frequently, workers pay into a 'Saturday fund', schemes where in return for a small weekly contribution people are given access to hospital, should they need it. And similar schemes operate all over the country for access to a GP, usually run by Friendly Societies or sick clubs. These schemes are very popular with working men, but working women and their families are often excluded from the schemes, so they cannot benefit from them.

THE COST OF SEEING A GP

GPs perform a wide range of services. In rural areas, they might practise surgery or deliver babies, as well as treating patients for minor complaints and prescribing medicines for a range of illnesses. Their fees vary considerably because they tend to charge according to the patient's financial situation. Some GPs charge from 2s 6d up to 10s 6d for a visit in 1917. For midwifery they charge from 1 guinea (£1, 1s) to five guineas (£5, 5s) for delivering a baby. But some early twentieth-century GPs build up practices by lowering their fees for working people to as little as one shilling or even sixpence per consultation.

THE REAL SHERLOCKS

Sir William Arbuthnot-Lane is a Scottish surgeon, regarded as the best abdominal surgeon in the country. He operates on Edwardian royalty, politicians and many society figures. He also sets up the first plastic and reconstructive surgery unit to cope with war injuries following World War I. Ahead of his time by many decades, after World War I he creates The New Health Society, to promote exercise and eating fruit, vegetables and bran to help bowel problems.

Both he and Joseph Bell, Scottish personal surgeon to Queen Victoria, are early pioneers in forensic pathology, emphasising the importance of making a close, detailed observation of a patient before making a diagnosis. To illustrate this, Bell takes a total stranger and, by observation, works out the person's job and their recent activities. Thanks to the skills of these two men, Arthur Conan Doyle, who has previously served as a clerk at the Royal Edinburgh

Infirmary, goes on to pen the acclaimed detective story of Sherlock Holmes – whom he admits is partly based on the observant work of these two eminent doctors.

THE DIET DOCTOR

One of the more popular dieting fads of 1910 is 'Fletcherism' a somewhat eccentric view of nutrition propagated by Horace Fletcher, a wealthy American who claims that all bodily weakness is a result of the way people eat their food.

Fletcher believes that food should be kept in the mouth and chewed until all the flavour has been taken out; this means chewing endlessly until the food is liquefied – and if it can't be reduced to liquid, it must be spat out. He also believes that the proof of this is greatly reduced bowel movements, claiming that he only goes to the toilet once a week or even once a fortnight. 'Munching parties' are held where the guests must spend five minutes chewing each small piece of food – and stopwatches are used to ensure the right amount of chewing. Even *The Lancet*, the esteemed British medical journal, endorses his principles. And for some, following Fletcherism does result in weight loss.

Here are some of his diet guidelines:
- eat no breakfast at all
- eat what you want, when you want it – provided you chew it properly
- keep a bowl of sugar lumps or candy on the dining table
- wine must be swilled around the mouth
- foods which dissolve quickly are of the greatest value

THE QUACK

In the early part of the twentieth century respiratory diseases are a major cause of death for both sexes, especially from illnesses like TB (often known as consumption).

Unscrupulous 'quacks' (an unqualified or fake doctor) sometimes advertise miracle cures for consumption to gullible newspaper readers. An American graduate from Michigan, Derk P Yonkerman, claims he has a treatment for TB by introducing copper into the blood in order to kill the bacilli; after selling the product, called Tuberculozyne, in the US, he launches it in the UK in 1903. The product costs £2,10s for a month's treatment and consists of two bottles of liquid: after each meal, the patient is advised to put thirty drops of each into a glass of milk, stir well and drink straight away. The British Medical Association analyses the liquids which are found to contain glycerine, potassium bromide, oil of cassis, tincture of capsicum, cochineal (to give a bright red colouring), oil of almond, sugar, water and a tiny amount of copper. Total cost of ingredients: two-and-a-half pence.

'Now, instead of the American public being fleeced by the English medical fakers, the American quack is finding the English public "good pickings",' says the American Medical Association publication, *Nostrums & Quackery*. Unfortunately, the US food and drug laws around advertising claims are more stringent than those in Britain at the time – so quacks like Derk Yonkerman can use these wildly exaggerated claims in his UK advertising – and fleece many unsuspecting sick people in search of a miracle cure.

THE BENEFIT CLUB

In 1902, The Dowager Countess of Scarborough founds The Sandbeck Nursing Association, a Benefit Club scheme for all those living in the community, where local working people contribute a nominal sum, according to their income, in order to access the services of a qualified nurse in their home. The cost is two shillings a year – half a penny a week – plus a one-off fee of two shillings and sixpence. 'The occurrence of illness in a family of the poorer classes usually finds the members of it destitute of the commonest sick appliances, ignorant of the simplest means of nursing and unconscious of preventable sanitary evils surrounding the patient,' says *The Tickhill Parish Magazine*, Doncaster. And thanks, in part, to the efforts of the lady of the manor, money collected at fund-raising events helps to fund Doncaster Royal Infirmary & Dispensary – so local people can access its in- and outpatient facilities.

CONTRACEPTION

Condoms made of animal gut have been in use since the nineteenth century and can be purchased by the wealthy. But they only start to be used by ordinary people during World War I when they are handed out to soldiers to lessen the effects of venereal disease. Early versions of diaphragms or Dutch caps (a protective device that a woman inserts into her vagina) are also available. But they are costly, ten shillings for a cap, unaffordable for ordinary working people. And given the strong moral attitudes against illegitimacy and unmarried sex, many still believe that such things are merely a licence for promiscuity. Although the term 'birth control' is coined by US contraception campaigner Margaret Sanger in 1914, contraception only starts to become more openly discussed in the twenties, following the opening of UK birth control campaigner Mary Stopes's family planning clinic in London in 1921.

VENEREAL DISEASE

Sexually transmitted diseases like syphilis and gonorrhea are rife at this time, as they have been for centuries. There are no known cures for what is called 'the French pox', closely associated with prostitutes and immoral sexuality. In Victorian times, some men believed that intercourse with a virgin child would actually cure venereal disease. Syphilis is sometimes treated with mercury, which is not always successful, yet there is no workable treatment for either gonorrhea or syphilis until the development of antibiotics many years later. A Royal Commission is set up in 1913 to enquire into the prevalence of venereal diseases; it advises more educational work and propaganda to help reduce the incidences of these illnesses. So when war breaks out in 1914, the distribution of contraceptives to soldiers becomes a priority to attempt to halt the spread of these diseases.

Many famous people are known to have contracted these sexually transmitted illnesses, including Henry VIII. And some historians claim that Winston Churchill's father, Lord Randolph Churchill, contracted syphilis as a young man in the red light district of Paris, one reason cited for the long 'together but apart' marriage with his wife, Jennie. Isabella Beeton, writing her famous *Book of Household Management* at the age of twenty one, is reputed to have contracted syphilis from her publisher husband, Sam, on their honeymoon; she dies, aged twenty eight, following the birth of their fourth child; there is some debate as to whether this was in fact the cause of her demise.

A LONGER LIFE

In 1911 there were 100 people aged 100 or over in UK; today there are 12,000 UK centenarians.

Cycling was a new form of recreation for the Edwardians at the start of the 20th Century.